AF701422

Revitalizing Cities

THE HRI VISION

REGIONS
LOEWS

Revitalizing Cities

The HRI Vision

Pres Kabacoff,
Eddie Boettner,
and Tom Leonhard

with James P. Farwell

University of Louisiana at Lafayette Press
2016

University of Louisiana at Lafayette Press
P.O. Box 40831
Lafayette, LA 70504-0831
http://ulpress.org

© 2016 by University of Louisiana at Lafayette Press
All rights reserved

ISBN 13 (hardcover): 978-1-935754-79-4

Printed in Canada.

Contents

GRUNEWALD'S
COSMOPOLITAN HOTEL
DRINK
CHATTANOOGA
BEER
LAZARD'S
MEN & BOYS OUTFITTERS
A.B. GRISWOLD & Co.
D.H. HOLMES CO. LTD.

Foreword

New Orleans is an old city that stands apart from many other American cities. It is a city of distinctive neighborhoods that are culturally diverse, an ethnic gumbo as rich as the wonderful cuisine for which south Louisiana and New Orleans are rightly renowned.

As someone who has long been involved in neighborhood issues and strongly supports historic revitalization, I long ago became interested in HRI Properties. Its co-founder, Pres Kabacoff, is a prominent figure in New Orleans. He's unusual in a lot of ways. A prosperous businessman and civic leader, he is as much an idealist as an entrepreneur. The story of how he and his partner, Edward B. Boettner, capitalized on the 1984 Louisiana World's Fair to spark a renaissance in the warehouse district upriver from the Central Business District is well known.

Ten years after Katrina provided an opportunity to look more closely at HRI's philosophy and what it had accomplished in revitalizing New Orleans. The company's mission is rooted in New Urbanism, an urban design movement that promotes walkable neighborhoods. In 1993, the Congress for New Urbanism articulated a charter that advocated neighborhoods with diverse populations, situated close to public transit and within walking distance to work, restaurants, shops, and other services. The resulting neighborhoods are places of beauty.

A thriving neighborhood requires density. One of the reasons Paris, Rome, London, and many other cities around the world have so many great places to live and work is that the population density is high enough to support offices, restaurants, and shops. Unlike many American cities, which so often are characterized by urban sprawl, the historic layout of New Orleans survived over the years. But by the 1990s, many historic buildings had become vacant or dilapidated. They faced a wrecking ball or "modern" plans for "urban renewal" from developers who lacked interest in or sensitivity to historic areas.

As it grew and expanded, HRI embarked upon an ambitious effort to channel its energies into fostering, in its words, diverse, vibrant, and sustainable communities. Pres and his team understood that architecture and landscape design should celebrate local history, climate, and building practice. They realized that density and pedestrian foot traffic made a neighborhood safer. Above all, they demonstrated aesthetic taste. HRI took pains to ensure that the properties it acquired and renovated respected their historical legacy.

Their mission extends beyond bringing the old to new life. Their approach, whether revitalizing the Woodward Wight Building, turning the old Blue Plate mayonnaise factory into affordable lofts for artists, or transforming heavily vacant public housing developments into mixed income, mixed use neighborhoods that offered new opportunity for residents, aimed like the sun to shine rays on the surrounding neighborhoods and infuse them with new vitality.

HRI's work is hardly confined to New Orleans. It has done landmark development in states from Texas to Nebraska, Mississippi to North Carolina. Its footprint stretches from coast to coast. Whether it is revitalizing a five story historic building or a skyscraper, its business philosophy remains consistent. It understands how to deliver top-tier projects that are financial successes. In short, it epitomizes the notion that a business can dramatically improve neighborhoods, cities, and communities while prospering. It's no surprise that investors and lenders find it interesting, pragmatic, and a good business partner.

HRI is more than interesting. It stands apart as a company that works hard to increase its bottom line, form prosperous business partnerships for growth, and maintain its role as a leading national real estate company while staying true to its mission rooted in the revitalization of historic properties.

The company is led by three individuals. Pres Kabacoff is a lawyer and New Urbanist intellectual who has a natural feel for urban design that draws people back from the suburbs to an inner city with new life, beautiful architecture whose scale and designs exude personality, and an atmosphere that infuses a city with interest and excitement.

Tom Leonhard represents the next generation of leadership. He epitomizes individuals who start from the bottom and make it to the top through energy, hard work, talent, and imagination. Warm and personable, he understands people and their passions, and he excels at running a business.

Eddie Boettner seems laid back when you meet him, but by the time he joined HRI he had already proven his mettle as a driving force in business, having established and sold a highly successful enterprise of his own. His tough-minded organizational and administrative skills are manifest throughout HRI's activities.

At left: Canal Street, New Orleans, La., circa 1905.

Leadership forges the vision, sets the tone, and defines the culture of a company. But any successful company owes its success to attracting a team that helps to develop the company's vision and to translate it into reality. Pres, Tom, and Eddie accomplished that. I had the pleasure of getting to know a lot of HRI's staff, and their enthusiasm, talent, and idealism at every level was striking.

This book looks at the history, philosophy, and approach to revitalization from HRI's perspective. Its work powerfully vindicates the view that cities should and can be not only livable but unique places of energy and excitement. HRI's accomplishments attest to that notion and provide tangible proof of its validity.

James P. Farwell,
January 2016

River Garden, the redeveloped St. Thomas Housing Project, New Orleans, La.

PREFACE

A Vision Driven by a Mission

This book illustrates the philosophy of HRI Properties, its core competencies, and its vision for the future. That philosophy drives what we do and how we do it. HRI opened its doors in 1982 to take advantage of the real estate market as people rethought where they wanted to live, work, and be entertained. In the years after World War II, what was termed "Drivable Suburban" areas dominated real estate development. Drivable suburban communities had low-density population. Cars and trucks connected them. Income and race separated housing, retail, office locations, and where people went for entertainment. This era gave birth to the modern suburb. Suburbs grew at the expense of city centers. In inner cities, historic buildings fell to the wrecking ball. Office buildings made vacant by modern skyscrapers were torn down to make way for parking lots. Multi-story warehouses became functionally obsolete and were also demolished.

WALKABLE URBAN NEIGHBORHOODS

As the twentieth century drew to a close, the pendulum shifted. Millenials without a family led the charge. Baby boomers wanted to live closer to cultural and entertainment attractions. Demand for living in a walkable urban environment inspired a return to city centers. People wanted to live, work, and be entertained in places to which they could walk. HRI perceived the shift early on. We developed our philosophy and defined our mission around that recognition. Today, a strong desire exists to reside in *walkable urban neighborhoods*.[1]

People want to live in neighborhoods that have high-density population, homes, shops, restaurants, museums, boutique retail hotels, and offices within walking distance of one another. They want to connect to these through different modes of transportation. Instead of driving, they want to walk or bicycle to destinations. For an old city like New Orleans, where HRI is headquartered, the quality of historic, walkable neighborhoods is integral to its physical lay-out and ethos. Our city is unique in many ways. But neighborhoods and communities with these characteristics are the new model for real estate development in the twenty-first century.

Environmental concerns accelerated this shift. Motor vehicles and buildings account for 70 percent of greenhouse gas emissions. Moving a household from the suburbs to a walkable urban community reduces household emissions by 50 to 80 percent. As transportation is at least 20 percent of most household budgets, such a move reduces the cost of living. In supporting the hard and soft infrastructure of "greener" communities, government seems likely to subsidize walkable neighborhoods, just as it had done so with drivable suburban communities by building the interstate highway system and providing home mortgage deductions.

Recent research as to migration trends in the Boston metropolitan area evidences the depth of desire across the nation for this new lifestyle.[2] Smart Growth America estimates that demand in Boston will equate to approximately one walkable community per 88,000 people in a metropolitan area of more than four million.[3] The walkability ratio will vary from city to city. It will depend on education levels, the underlying need to create significant centers of economic vitality, and community attitudes towards permitting growth.[4] Yet "nimbyism"—opposition by residents to a proposal for a new development because it is close to them—discourages commercial development essential for these neighborhoods to grow into significant centers for economic vitality.

Cities have different categories of neighborhoods that will attract and accommodate the new national migration. These include Downtown-Historic centers that are located next to former light-industrial and warehouse buildings; areas that are distinct from urban centers; areas generally near urban centers that are home to universities, hospitals, and museums; and suburban town centers that are walkable.

COMMUNITY REVITALIZATION

Community revitalization is a complex process. Barriers to entry are high. It mandates clear focus upon "hard" infrastructure such as public transportation, drainage, roads, streetscapes, and parks. It demands equal attention to "soft" infrastructure. Soft infrastructure embraces the creation of vision and a development plan. One must bring key stakeholders to the table who participate in the process. A development plan must define the roles of the public and non-profits. It must enable healthy public/private partnerships—more accurately *private/public* partnerships, as the private sector provides 80 percent of the capital and the talent required to bring a complex real estate development to realization.

The key player on the private side is a *catalytic development company*. This party must have the experience and capacity to lead project development. A good one works with its public and nonprofit partners to put the hard and soft infrastructure in place. It implements a real estate strategy. It delivers the core elements that comprise a community. Those include apartments, hotels, offices, retail, and places of entertainment.

Achieving success requires leadership and vision. In the 1980s, HRI had to persuade banks and investors to finance the adaptive reuse of historic buildings into market rate and affordable residential housing. During the 1990s, we convinced lenders to finance the adaptive reuse of historic buildings for full service hotels. Later we persuaded banks to finance the adaptive reuse of historic buildings for focused service hotels. Eventually banks and investors were persuaded to finance the conversion of public housing projects into mixed-income housing. HRI convinced the federal government to utilize Low Income Housing Tax Credits for artist housing. After showing the public benefits, HRI convinced state governments to create tax incentives to convert historic buildings into new commercial and residential uses.

More recently, we convinced lenders and investors to finance the adaptive reuse of a single, large historic building into a mixed use of hotel, residences, retail, and parking.

DIVERSE, VIBRANT, SUSTAINABLE COMMUNITIES

As a private business, HRI exists to earn a profit. Still, we stand distinct from real estate companies by our mission: *Revitalize cities by creating diverse, vibrant, sustainable communities*.

What does that mean? Let's break it down.

Revitalizing cities means a focus on walkable urban communities connected to public transit rather than sprawling suburban neighborhoods. Why focus on cities? They are the central gathering place for interaction between people to share knowledge. Historically, infrastructure has already been created and there's no need to build it from scratch. Cities get people out of their cars and affords walkable access to places where they live, work, and play.

> **Diverse** means walkable neighborhoods that contain a mix of real estate products, uses (residences, offices, shops, and restaurants, for instance), and income levels.
>
> **Vibrant** means neighborhoods that exude the joy and excitement that flow from a sense of place.
>
> **Sustainable** means neighborhoods that civically, socially, and environmentally are built to last.

Creating is the operative word that sets HRI apart. HRI will capitalize on opportunities as they appear in urban centers. As urban centers mature, the markets become highly competitive and properties become expensive. That is not an obstacle for HRI. Its vision and capacity to actualize it enables us to create opportunities in blighted neighborhoods that have concentrated poverty and failed infrastructure. HRI is a catalytic developer. We work in partnership with government to revitalize entire neighborhoods. This approach creates opportunities for cities and their residents and propels HRI to new business successes.

LEADING THE WAY

HRI and its principals have applied these precepts in leading the revitalization of entire neighborhoods through public/private partnerships. In New Orleans, HRI projects have included the Warehouse District, historic Central Business District, Mid-City, the former St. Thomas and Iberville public housing projects, Lower Canal Street, Algiers, and St. Claude Corridor. Outside Louisiana, they include the urban centers of Dallas, Houston, Jackson, Minneapolis, Nashville, Philadelphia, Richmond, St. Louis, and Winston-Salem.
We deeply believe our work makes an important, positive contribution to society. We take our mission seriously. Jim Collins's seminal work, *Built to Last*, confirms that companies with strong core ideologies that benefit communities last longer, out-perform the competition, and provide a greater financial return. We are passionate about our work. We believe we excel at revitalizing cities by creating diverse, vibrant, and sustainable communities.

Kurt Weigle, the President and CEO of the New Orleans Downtown Development District, has aptly summarized HRI's approach:

> HRI is known for taking on projects that other folks shy away from. They take on projects that require creative financing. They take on projects that have a strong social benefit. One example is their work in creating mixed-income housing. They pay attention not just to the confines of their buildings, but they think deeply about how their projects will actually react with the neighborhoods and how the project can contribute to the neighborhood. They look at what needs to happen in the public realm in order to create a healthier, and more vibrant neighborhood.[5]

Pres Kabacoff,
January 2016

INTRODUCTION

Vibrant Communities

Americans are in the middle of a structural change in how we build our country. We invest over 35 percent of our wealth in the built environment (infrastructure and real estate), the largest asset class in the economy. Starting in the mid-1990s, we have been gradually investing in a fundamentally different way than in the last half of the twentieth century. We are shifting from "drivable sub-urban" habitation, which is low density, single product type living segregated by use, income, and race, connected only by cars and trucks. The new approach, actually a modern version of thousands of years of development traditions, is "walkable urban"—high density, multiple product type-living with integrated uses, income, and race, connected to other places by many transportation systems (automobile, truck, rail and bus, bike and pedestrian), and walkable.

There have been very few real estate pioneers in the rediscovery of walkable urban development. These include publicly traded Real Estate Investment Trust (REITs) such as Federal Realty, Post Properties, Equity Residential, AvalonBay, Boston Properties, and, just converted to a REIT, Forest City Enterprises. Most have been private entities, such as Hines Interests, Related, Rose Associates, McCormack Baron Salazar, CityView, Jair Lynch Real Estate Partners, and the focus of this book, HRI Properties.

Beginning in the 1980s, well before most of the above companies ever heard of walkable urbanism, HRI began developing in then-abandoned city centers. Starting in New Orleans, but expanding to small and large towns in Texas, Mississippi, Missouri, Nebraska, Minnesota, Pennsylvania, Tennessee, and Virginia, among other states, HRI took this rediscovered development approach national. Mastering walkable urbanism early provided HRI with a unique competitive advantage that continues in many metro areas where the local development community has yet to understand it or its necessary changes fully.

HRI's adoption of a walkable urban approach is probably due to the unique character of its hometown. Unlike the majority of American cities that completely abandoned their center cities, New Orleans never lost its walkable urban heritage. This is due in part to the Spanish and French cultural history of the city and the subsequent economic role of a tourism industry based upon walkable urbanism. Except for the Interstate 10 system, it did not blast highways through its core, though there was still considerable "urban renewal" and, by the early 1980s, a significant number of abandoned warehouses, historic office buildings, and department stores. It was the repurposing of these warehouses, redevelopment of historic buildings, and revitalization of public housing into mixed-income developments that the then-named Historic Restoration, Inc., set about to achieve.

HRI's co-founder, Pres Kabacoff, is one of walkable urbanism's true pioneers. I first met him in the early 1990s after he read some of my articles and books about this structural shift. Every time we met or talked over the years, he would invariably ask, "what else can I read about New Urbanism and walkable urbanism?" As an early adaptor of this new development approach, he also brought on board the senior executives needed to implement that vision, such as Tom Leonhard, Edward B. Boettner, and Boettner's his son, Eddie, who replaced his father after his passing to make sure that vision would be implemented on the ground.

Walkable urbanism is fundamentally different than drivable sub-urban development. Those differences include the development of multiple transportation systems, site acquisition, construction, marketing, and project management. However, there are three aspects of walkable urban development that are most strikingly dissimilar from drivable sub-urban: place management, financing, and social and environmental concerns.

Place management refers to the care and management of a walkable urban place, referred to as a WalkUP for short. WalkUPs tend to be one hundred to five hundred acres in size and could be original downtowns, downtown-adjacent places surrounding the original, urban commercial districts, urban universities, suburban town centers, drivable sub-urban malls and business parks, or green/brown field developments. HRI tends to focus on downtown and downtown-adjacent WalkUPs. Place management involves the safety and cleanliness of these areas; their festivals, economic development, and infrastructure; and the pedestrian-level experience.

Place management is a missing level of governance in our society, supplementing federal, state, and local government. Most place management occurs through private sector business improvement districts (BIDs), although there are other organizational options as well—in New Orleans, it's the Downtown Development District. HRI has been actively involved with place management either through established BIDs or, in some cases, as the place manager outright if their holdings are large enough, such as the downtown-adjacent Iberville/Tremé neighborhoods in New Orleans.

Place management is concerned with defining and maintaining the unique character and economic function of a WalkUP. It involves the safety and cleanliness, festivals, economic development, infrastructure, and the pedestrian level experience of the WalkUP, managing it on a 24/7 basis. Most place management is private sector business improvement districts (BIDs), although there are other organizational options as well. HRI has been actively involved with place management either through established BIDs or in some cases they act as the place manager if their holdings are large enough, such as downtown adjacent Iberville/Tremé neighborhoods in New Orleans.

Since walkable urban places perform differently, they require a different approach to financing. Drivable sub-urban development destroys the very features that are its original appeal—ease of commuting by car, open space, and environmental cleanliness. As more is built, these factors diminish, which is the primary reason sprawl has continued further out to the fringe of metropolitan areas. It can be described as *more is less* development. The short-term nature of the economic returns from drivable sub-urbanism result in the demand for short-term financial results, generally with a three- to seven-year time horizon. At the end of the useful life of drivable sub-urban development, the asset is either rebuilt if it is still economically viable or it is sold to an owner that will under-invest, leading to a gradual decline in value as sprawl moves demand further to the fringe.

On the other hand, additional walkable urban development in a WalkUP adds value over time. As more retail, housing, and office space is added, it puts more people on the street, increasing safety and vitality, as well as retail sales, rents/housing prices, property values, and taxes. In other words, *more is better*. The governor of the amount of development in a WalkUP is the distance people are willing to walk, generally 1,500 to 3,000 feet, which keeps overbuilding under control much better than in drivable sub-urban locations. Successful WalkUPs create a virtual spiral of value creation.

Walkable urban development costs more, however, this is due to better architecture and construction that is immediately adjacent to the customer on the sidewalk, not set back by 150 feet of surface parking. The foundations of these structures are more substantial and the construction type is more costly. Parking must be decked, either above ground or, even more expensively, below ground, though less parking is required per square foot of occupied space. The financing of walkable urban development must account for higher upfront costs, but economic performance is more robust in the mid- to long-term (seven to forty years).

Finally, walkable urban development is required to address the two most important issues in contemporary America—the lack of mixed-income development and climate change. Many walkable urban projects receive special incentives from local government and, in exchange, generally provide affordable housing. The building of walkable urban places has recently been shown to be the most effective means by which to lower green house gas emissions; walkable places use far less fossil fuel for transportation and high density buildings are far more energy efficient.

Urban centers with historic fabric and connected to public transportation have attracted millennials to live, tourists to visit, and offices that had decamped to the suburbs to return. HRI has been leading the country in understanding how to build complex walkable urban projects and places. Based in walkable urban New Orleans and working throughout the country, they learned the lessons of walkable urbanism before the vast majority of the real estate industry, much of which is still stuck in the late twentieth-century model of drivable sub-urbanism. The management of HRI understands that achieving a "triple bottom line"–economic returns, social equity, and environmental sustainability–is required in the urbanizing twenty-first century. As this book will demonstrate using on-the-ground examples, HRI has not only learned these lessons but applied them to create a sustainable company that cities across the country compete for to develop and oversee long-term, prosperous projects in their jurisdictions.

HRI's early mastering of walkable urban development gives them a unique competitive advantage in the twenty-first century, one that only a few national companies can claim.

Christopher B. Leinberger
Locus, President;
Brookings Institution, Nonresident Senior Fellow;
George Washington University School of Business,
Charles Bendit Distinguished Scholar and Research Professor;
Arcadia Land Company, Founding Partner

HRI Properties

Vibrancy restored - the River Garden residential development, New Orleans, La.

CREATING DIVERSE, VIBRANT, SUSTAINABLE COMMUNITIES
by Tom Leonhard and Eddie Boettner

HRI is a rising leader in the real estate development industry. It has commanded respect and recognition by carrying out a well-defined mission to create vibrant, diverse, sustainable communities. It is a company whose business model revitalizes historic properties into walkable urban neighborhoods, is profitable, and benefits communities. The success this model enjoys can be repeated consistently and profitably. What has been achieved in New Orleans can be achieved in top-tier cities and communities across the United States.

HRI Properties, LLC[6] got started in 1982 in New Orleans. These were uncertain times. In company with other beleaguered cities like Detroit, Gary, and Newark, New Orleans was spiraling downwards. HRI founders Pres Kabacoff and Edward B. Boettner succeeded in creating a successful company with a practical vision that combined profitable business and community revitalization.

Working with the preservationist community, HRI poured energy and determination into bringing the blighted Warehouse District of New Orleans back to life. From there it shifted focus and successively helped to revitalize areas of Canal Street, Mid-City, the lower Garden District, the historic Central Business District, Bywater, Algiers, Gert Town, and today, Upper Canal and Tremé.

HRI prides itself on being a learning company that actively seeks out and acts on innovative new ideas. It has taken on the complex dynamics of mixed-income, elderly, and artist housing and learned how to generate public assistance to make projects that foster economic revitalization possible. Mastering a diverse skill set, particularly in historic preservation, has proven central to its success and sets it apart.

When a brutal recession struck the nation in the mid-1980s, HRI's acumen enabled it to prosper while competitors shut down. The company has continually broadened the scope of its work. It ranks among the few development companies in the nation to receive New Market Tax Credits. In renewing communities, it has emerged as a national thought leader in the New Urbanist movement, a key component of which is the notion of walkable neighborhoods. None of this went unnoticed. Even during HRI's early days, Ernst & Young honored its unique standing, awarding the company the prestigious Entrepreneur of the Year award for the nation. In the real estate industry, winning that award is like winning an Oscar for Best Picture. It was an exciting moment and came as a stunning surprise.

HRI became a great company because it has had the right leadership, hired the right team, and forged and executed a realistic vision for success. We bet on the recovery and revitalization of an iconic city. The company is built to last with a reputation for excellence. Our entrepreneurial spirit and vertically integrated team of 2,000 individuals have made HRI a company that spurs creativity as it builds communities through revitalization. We respect those whom our projects affect, deliver on time and within budget, and value the opinions of stakeholders. Our approach to earning profits while benefitting communities underscores a vision that is both pragmatic and idealistic.

THE HRI BRAND AND IDENTITY

HRI's brand and identity are rooted in its key pillars: vision, culture, excellence, trusted relationships, and community commitment. We pursue a well-defined mission geared to market realities, staying power, and profitable operations. The company is a proven success, doing over $2.5 billion of top quality projects spread across different states. We revitalize buildings as a catalyst to renew surrounding neighborhoods and communities. Now we're taking that proven success at the community and business levels to renew and revitalize top-tier cities across the country.

Restored St. Roch Market, symbol of the revived Bywater neighborhood.

THE BEGINNINGS OF HRI PROPERTIES

When Edward B. Boettner and Pres Kabacoff founded HRI Properties in 1982, their goal was to adaptively reuse and restore empty warehouse buildings in New Orleans's historic Warehouse District. For years, the Port of New Orleans, the second largest in the U.S. throughout its history, had enabled the district to thrive. But that was vanishing. Logistical considerations driven by the shift from cargo to containers drove the shipping business to new locations up and down river. The Warehouse District had been suffering from blight and abandonment.

The six-month 1984 Louisiana World Exposition, held one hundred years after the city's 1884 World Cotton Centennial, sparked a renaissance. The modern theme was "The World of Rivers—Fresh Waters as a Source of Life." The mascot, a blue and white costume pelican with large eyes and a huge, yellow beak named Seymore D. Fair, epitomized its festive spirit. Despite unexpectedly low attendance, the exposition thrilled and entertained New Orleans area residents.

The fair captured the imagination of HRI and other developers. Patty Gay, Executive Director of the Preservation Resource Center, explains the background:

> For most of the nineteenth century, New Orleans was among the nation's five largest cities. That gave the city a historic built environment that was more substantial than other cities, and that had survived "urban renewal" and other programs more than most cities, anchored as it was by the French Quarter. Other cities were tearing down their inner city buildings for high-rise buildings, and for the most part had little if any residential use downtown. We are the only large city in the country that has its original city—the French Quarter. The architecture was there.
>
> The Fair presented a very positive focus on the city, which, like all cities, had been losing population, especially in the inner city. It gave us the opportunity to capitalize on the thriving French Quarter, protected by the Vieux Carré Commission since 1936, that had maintained its residential use and character. The Fair, along with the federal rehabilitation tax credit, established in 1981, stimulated investor interest and interest in living above Canal Street—into Lafayette Square, Picayune Place, and the Warehouse District. Additionally, in 1983, the PRC had published a study of the Warehouse District, funded by the National Trust for Historic Preservation, in which we urgently promoted the preservation of the district as opposed to speculative demolition.
>
> The World's Fair could have resulted in the leveling of the district. In other cities, that's probably what would have happened. Preservationists in many capacities worked to instill a general awareness of the real potential in historic neighborhoods. And suddenly it was all logical. The Fair, the tax credit, and the PRC/NTHP study established a strong preservation ethic for the Warehouse District. Entrepreneurs like Pres, Ed, and Gerry Derks and others, with their bold willingness to take action, showed that business supported it as well. And HRI never stopped, continues to this day to do exciting projects throughout the city, even out of state.[7]

HOW THE WORLD'S FAIR CAME TO NEW ORLEANS

Public Affairs Research Executive Director Ed Stagg approached Lester Kabacoff with the idea of having New Orleans designated a site for a Category 2 World's Fair.[8] The goals were to improve a section of New Orleans and increase tourism during the heat of the summer. They selected the Warehouse District as the site, hoping the Fair would revitalize it.

Unfortunately, the world was entering an oil and gas recession. Persuading businesses from different nations to lease space and operate pavilions proved difficult. In 1980, the federal government had sunk nearly a quarter of a billion dollars into the Knoxville World's Fair. It committed a paltry $10 million to the New Orleans Fair. The responsibility thus fell on New Orleans businesses to dip into their own pocketbooks to fund the Fair's pre-development. They hoped that robust attendance would repay their investments.

The year it was held, the New Orleans World's Fair failed to improve summer tourism. Management had forecast thirteen million visitors and predicated the financial feasibility of the Fair on that assumption. Only half that many showed up.

Lacking major government subsidies, the New Orleans World's Fair lost $100 million and was deemed a failure. But New Orleans's businesses that funded the event unwittingly made an investment in urban renewal. Their investment had a far-reaching impact, achieving the Fair's broader goal of revitalization. Today the Warehouse District is thriving. It ranks among the hottest, most desirable areas in the nation. It's a vibrant community, boasting over 3,500 residents and 250 new businesses. An upsurge of museums, galleries, restaurants, hotels, and residences mark the neighborhood.

What's the lesson? It is that the significance of a World's Fair lies less in its financial success for the period that it is open than what it leaves behind. By that measure the New Orleans Fair was a resounding success and a catalyst for urban renewal. HRI managed to capitalize on the Fair's long-term success.

THE COMPANY

HRI's work is complex. To manage it, HRI has vertically integrated its team to include "in-house" city planning and government relations; development and finance; architecture, interior design, and construction management; and hotel and apartment management. HRI has built a strong team by placing the right people in the right places. Vice President of Human Resources Dione Heusel rightly has stated that its mission:

> moves beyond the restoration of the beautiful buildings, decorative façades, and interesting architecture to the way people live their lives as they create closely knit societies. Our employees provide the foundation for such success. They form the HRI community. They create an environment that fosters excellence. We attract top people. We nurture their individual talents much as we respect the unique originality of buildings that our team restores. We provide our employees challenging and engaging work.

They are cohesive, gifted, and passionate about HRI's work, and they foster a healthy work environment. In 2014, *City Business* named HRI as New Orleans's best place to work. Over the last four years running, it has ranked HRI among the top ten best places to work.

A NATIONAL PLAYER FOR REVITALIZATION

HRI specializes in the art and science of revitalizing neighborhoods through public/private partnerships. It has completed seventy major projects comprising $2.5 billion in development. That depth accords HRI the capacity to pursue a wide range of projects that produce walkable communities and to sustain robust development during the inevitable downturns of the real estate cycle.

Headquartered in New Orleans, HRI is a national player. The head of its investment team, Michael Coolidge, has well described their goal: "We want to be the company that people want to work with because they admire and respect our work ethic, values, and ability to get things accomplished, delivering the highest quality of work on time and within budget."

HRI is growing, and it sustains this growth through three platforms: third party management and technical service agreements; acquisitions and joint ventures; and new development in walkable communities.

CREATING MAJOR ECONOMIC IMPACT

HRI has completed major projects in Baton Rouge, Dallas, Ft. Worth, Hammond, Houma, Houston, Jackson, Lafayette, New Iberia, Omaha, Richmond, St. Louis, Shreveport, and Winston-Salem. These include 5,114 apartment units, 4,116 hotel rooms, and 1,300,000 square feet of office and rental space. The funding value of these projects exceeds $2.5 billion.

A 2012 study by Dr. Tim Ryan of the University of New Orleans revealed that since its inception, "HRI . . . contributed $19.53 billion in present value terms to the economy of New Orleans and generated tax revenues that have a 2012 value of $942.73 million in economic impact for the city of New Orleans."[9]

AWARD WINNING WORK

HRI's work has won numerous awards. These include awards from the Louisiana Landmarks Society for Excellence in Historic Preservation; the Locus Leadership Award; the Downtown Development District of New Orleans's award for Best Downtown Development Project; the National Preservation Honor Award; the McGraw Hill Best of the Best award for Best Specialty Project & Best Architecture; the Mississippi Heritage Trust's Heritage Award for Excellence; the Downtown St. Louis Partnership Cityscape Award; the Design-Build Institute of American Merit Award; the Urban Land Institute Award for Excellence; the Landmarks Association of St. Louis Inc.'s Eleven Most Enhanced Sites Award; the Hyatt and Hilton Best Hotel Development; and many others.

FIXED ON THE FUTURE

HRI's vision reflects its deep commitment to building a brighter future for those its projects affect. Its philosophy is rooted in creating diverse, vibrant and sustainable communities. It defines who HRI is, what it stands for, and what it hopes to achieve.

Federal Fibre Mills, New Orleans, La.

FOUNDING THE COMPANY
by Pres Kabacoff

When I graduated from LSU law school, I went to work as an associate at Sessions Fishman law firm. My father, Lester Kabacoff—everybody called him Kabby—was Of Counsel. Besides practicing law, he was developing real estate. Beau Chene and International River Center stood out among his projects. It was my introduction to the business.

BEAU CHENE

New Orleans reached its peak in population in the early 1960s, with 647,000 residents before desegregation largely prompted white flight.[10] Initially, people moved to the adjoining parishes of Jefferson and St. Bernard and the city of Slidell and its surrounding area in St. Tammany Parish. In addition, Covington and Mandeville, located on the north shore of Lake Pontchartrain, proved a magnet for upper income residents.

Beau Chene arose from such an opportunity. U.S. Senator Russell Long had purchased a large tract of property in Mandeville. Unsure how to develop it, Long sought my father's counsel. My father had seen Hilton Head, a recreational residential community on the coast of South Carolina. Seeing opportunity, he and his partner, homebuilder Morgan Earnest, purchased the senator's land.

Louisiana's first oil shock in 1973 came just as we opened Beau Chene and began selling lots. We had invested $5 million, most of it borrowed capital. That's real money today, but in 1973, it was really big bucks. The oil shock raised major obstacles. Gas shortages left people lined up at gas stations. Nobody wanted to make a long commute. Lots were not selling. We were in serious straits. Happily, the banks believed in my father and his partner. They stuck with them. Otherwise, the oil shock would have taken them down. Today Beau Chene is a vibrant community for three thousand residents, filled with beautiful homes and amenities.

This project taught me fundamental lessons about real estate development, the real estate cycle, and migratory trends. Demand in Beau Chene was driven by a desire by middle and upper income persons to migrate out of the city. By 2005, NOLA had dropped to 465,000 residents. Such migration afflicted cities across our nation, including Newark, Gary, St. Louis, and Detroit. For these cities, as well as New Orleans, this resulted in a concentration of the poor.

The social implications of migration soon became apparent. Losing middle and upper income population impoverishes an inner city and creates a vicious downward cycle. Exiting taxpayers leave behind a poor population that lacks the earning power to pay for needed social services. The result is growing social malaise: bad schools, child abuse, single moms, and safety issues, which prompts even more taxpayer flight. For New Orleans, this dilemma persisted until a different tragedy struck in the form of Hurricane Katrina. Paradoxically, the storm reversed the city's fortunes and provided it with a fresh start.

Pres Kabacoff and Edward B. Boettner.

The New Orleans Warehouse District in 1974, a decade before its revival.

INTERNATIONAL RIVER CENTER AND CONVENTION CENTER

My father had a vision to rebuild the Riverfront. Warehouses and railroad tracks had isolated this area from the public. As with most cities, our waterway was used for transportation corridors and warehousing. Today, you can easily walk to the Mississippi River, but that was not the case in the 1970s.

Transformational projects that fundamentally change a city require public-private partnerships. In twentieth-century New Orleans, these types of projects included the Superdome, the Riverfront development, and decades ago during the 1930s, filling in parts of Lake Pontchartrain to create the lakefront. Transformational projects can bring long-term negative consequences. The interstate highway system accelerated flight from New Orleans. The proposed Riverfront expressway, the ill-conceived brainchild of New York power broker Robert Moses,[11] would have been a disaster for the French Quarter and other neighborhoods. Only the courage and perseverance of preservationists like Bill Borah and Martha Robinson stopped that ill-judged initiative. A well known attorney, Borah observes that:

> In 1946, the Louisiana Highway Department retained the services of Robert Moses, and the notorious freeway planner recommended the construction of an elevated expressway along the Vieux Carré riverfront. Moses' study was the product of a mindset that forgot that cities were for people rather than automobiles. Such thinking pervaded America at this time and city after city mistakenly turned their pedestrian-scaled neighborhoods into architectural wastelands of paved roads and parking lots. Downtown Los Angeles is seen as the classic example of this approach to urban planning.
>
> The Central Area Committee of the Chamber of Commerce embraced the finding of the Moses Report in 1957, and the effort to build the freeway began. From the outset the preservation community opposed the elevated freeway because they thought the six-lane highway would irreparably harm Jackson Square and the historic Vieux Carré. In 1969, Secretary of Transportation John A. Volpe announced that the Nixon Administration refused to fund the highway because it 'would have seriously impaired the historic quality of New Orleans' famed French Quarter,' thus ending what has become known as the Second Battle of New Orleans.
>
> If the Vieux Carré Riverfront Expressway, and its planned extension upriver through Audubon Park, had been built it would have created a Chinese Wall, forever separating the city from the river—the city's lifeblood and the very reason for its existence. So much of what we see today, or have seen in the recent past, would not exist or have existed. No pathway along the river in front of Jackson Square, no riverfront green space, no streetcar line, no aquarium, and no serious port expansion upriver. And how would the city have staged a World's Fair along the waterfront if that space was occupied by six lanes of concrete? And what about the six-lane bridge crossing the Mississippi that was slated to tie into the expressway at Napoleon Avenue, and the impact that approach system and flow of automobiles would have had on the pedestrian scale and character of Uptown New Orleans?
>
> As we look back in time and see what has been built and what could have been built along the city's riverfront, and the impact that some of that development has had and could have had on adjoining neighborhoods, we easily see why the preservation community celebrates the defeat of the Riverfront Expressway as if it was yesterday. Cities are for people, not automobiles, and the defeat of the Vieux Carré Riverfront Expressway, in the mind of preservationists, affirmed that principle—affirmed it for the citizens of New Orleans and affirmed it for all visitors drawn to the city because of its 'quaint and distinctive' character.[12]

In contrast, the transformation of sixty acres of Riverfront property from Poydras Street upriver to the Mississippi River Bridge that included the New Orleans Hilton Hotel and the Convention Center has proven a boon. Realizing that vision required a public/private partnership. My father and Jimmy Coleman Jr. led the team that developed the Hilton. The team included major railroads that owned property on the river. The key to making the project work was a land swap with the city, which owned the streets. Mayor Moon Landrieu negotiated a deal through which the private side received twenty acres from Poydras to Julia Streets and developed the Hilton. The public side got forty acres from Julia to the bridge on which the Convention Center was built. It was a great deal that produced a win-win for everyone.

New Orleans Convention Center, with Riverwalk entrance to the left.

1984 New Orleans World's Fair.

Getting the new Convention Center was a complicated public process. My father, who was a member of the New Orleans Tourist Commission, had travelled to Houston, where he noticed that the Astrodome and its convention facilities were attracting large conventions and tourists—tourists he believed would prefer the Crescent City. The venue that then served conventions was the Rivergate Exhibition Center, designed by the distinguished architect Arthur Davis, who also designed the Superdome. It was a modernist landmark, with a sweeping, curved roof and vast interior spaces. Unfortunately, with only 147,000 square feet, it was too small to attract large conventions.

The tourism community approached my father about getting a new convention center. One thing seemed certain—the Superdome had experienced huge cost over-runs that angered legislators. Securing public funding for a new center was going to be tough. With that reality in mind, they urged that the new Convention Center be constructed at the Poydras Street wharf, located on the river next to the Hilton Hotel. Mayor Dutch Morial held a different view. He insisted that the city required not just a new but larger facility. A powerful, commanding figure who dominated the New Orleans political scene, nobody did anything in politics without first asking "where's Dutch on this?" Morial persuaded the tourism folks to sign onto his approach.

Obtaining funding took getting an agreement between Mayor Morial and Senate President Mike O'Keefe; each a legendary political powerhouse. O'Keefe's nickname was "the spider," because he knew every fiber in the web of connections out of which the state's political fabric was spun. He was so subtle in his adroit use of power that everyone said he could walk on snow without leaving tracks. Unfortunately, these two often did not see eye-to-eye. Happily, this time, they worked together. Their efforts led to the creation by the legislature of the Louisiana Exposition Authority and passage of a 1 percent hotel-motel tax. The tax proceeds were dedicated to funding construction of the new convention center. Unfortunately, the 1 percent was insufficient to complete the new facility. My father and Governor Dave Treen solved the problem of obtaining state funding for the first phase of the Convention Center by designating it as the Louisiana pavilion for the World's Fair.

THE WORLD'S FAIR AND FEDERAL FIBRE MILLS

The 1984 Louisiana World Exposition—known locally as the World's Fair—occupies a legendary place in the hearts of New Orleans residents. Ed Stagg of the Louisiana Public Affairs Research Council (PAR) approached my father with the idea. Pointing to successful world fairs around the world, Stagg suggested that my dad help promote one for New Orleans. I became heavily involved in this effort. It was one of the most exciting—and sometimes nerve-wracking—episodes in my career. There's not a roller coaster in the world that can jolt you with such steep highs and treacherous lows.

We decided to locate the fair in the Warehouse District, taking advantage of vacancy and blight. My role focused on assembling the eighty-eight-acre site. It was an ideal location. The district ranked among the three significant districts that comprised Downtown New Orleans, along with the French Quarter and the Central Business District.[13]

The possibilities fired my imagination. I had traveled to Soho in New York and the North End of Boston. I saw how these cities were converting industrial buildings and warehouses into homes. The beauty of the renovations registered: high ceilings, old brick, massive columns and beams, huge windows with light pouring in.

It was at this time that I met Edward B. Boettner. Ed was a successful businessman who had retired from the printing business. He was a savvy entrepreneur who understood finance and the value of historic incentives for real estate development. He was tough—he understood that just because you didn't have a solution to a pressing problem in sight didn't mean no solution existed; you just had to find it. Steeled by resolve, he viewed each tomorrow with an inspiring confidence, certain that new opportunities would present themselves. We made a great team.

Artist's rendering of the Federal Fibre Mills building at the 1984 World's Fair.

Federal Fibre Mills, New Orleans, La. , circa 1950.

I had an aesthetic vision, and I've always been blessed with tons of energy. In 1982, we purchased the Fibre Mills building, subject to the World's Fair lease. Fibre Mills enabled us to work with the World's Fair organization to establish an entertainment pavilion for the fair. Our long-term vision was to create the first residential development in the Warehouse District in a hundred years. The path to success was fraught with obstacles that scared the hell out of me. For example, the World's Fair had a six-month life, and the fair simply needed the building for entertainment. It only budgeted for temporary improvements. That was fine for them; in the long term, that investment would be wasted. We proposed to the fair that we supplement the fair's budget to make the Fibre Mills improvements permanent, an idea they happily agreed to.

We explored different options to make our pavilion work. I flew to Montreal to meet with a German family, the Racks, who had operated a famous beer garden in the 1967 Montreal World's Fair and had continued operating after that fair had ended. The Racks were an ideal candidate for our project. Partnering with them, we created a beer garden on the first floor of the building. Afterwards, I went to Jed Palmer, the owner and operator of Jed's, one of the best music nightclubs in New Orleans. He was a colorful character who reminded me of the protagonist in Hunter Thompson's great book, *Fear and Loathing in Las Vegas*. Intellectually conservative, he used to hold court at his bars and strongly espouse his political views. He was also a legendary carouser. Growing up in a soul town, I had long harbored the fantasy of owning a nightclub that featured live music and now I saw my big chance. We established Jed's Lookout on the second floor of the Fibre Mills building, complete with a balcony that looked out over the monorail traversing the fair grounds. To make the pavilion more indigenous to New Orleans, we used small buildings located in the courtyard for Cajun music and dancing and created a blacksmith shop.

But our eye was fixed on the road ahead. Our planned residential use for Fibre Mills was to create ten model apartments on the third floor. During the fair, we could rent them out as hospitality suites. Afterwards, we would fill them as residential apartments as part of the larger complex. As no one had lived in the neighborhood for a hundred years, the fair provided the opportunity needed to bring people into the area and see that this building could be a great place to live.

Inevitably in real estate development, the experience is exciting but also nerve-wracking. The Fair went bankrupt. We had funded big improvements but failed to get repaid. Instead of getting a leg up, we broke one. Our concessions were not financially successful. People in the city thought the fair the Greatest Show on Earth. But a side story illuminates why developers can end up with ulcers.

The World's Fair opened on May 11, 1984. Its executive director, Peter Spurney, insisted I be present in New Orleans for opening day. While the public was filled with mounting anticipation, I was a nervous wreck.

A week before the fair opened, Arnold Kagan was forecasting financial disaster. News like that does not bolster morale. I had no idea what he was talking about. But I *knew* that he knew. Kagan had held concessions in every World's Fair since 1936. He knew his stuff. Sadly, Kagan proved correct. Local jubilation for the fair masked the onset of a depression driven by a drop in the price of oil from fifty dollars to eight dollars a barrel. The depression cost Louisiana fifty thousand jobs.

Survival required that we move quickly to obtain the additional financing required to complete the renovation of Fibre Mills into Soho-type loft apartments. We were fast running out of money. Making payroll each week was always an issue. We knocked ourselves out to persuade lenders to finance the next development phase.

This was a nightmarish challenge. We had to show that we would obtain 95 percent occupancy at a square foot rate of ninety cents. Lenders knew that the oil shock had left 40 percent of apartment units vacant and that average rents had dropped to fity cents per square foot. No less than fifty lenders gave us the cold shoulder.

Our backs were against the wall. Invariably, the stouthearted Ed had faith. He was sure we'd find a solution. He proved right. They say that half of life is showing up. As we racked our brains, I remembered a Philadelphia company, Historic Landmarks for Living. It was the biggest developer of historic properties in the country. I called its CEO Stephen Solms, an unusual character with a beard who wore red shoes and big red-framed eyeglasses. I extolled our project while explaining that all we needed was a powerhouse company like his to bring it home. Intrigued, he asked for a package.

Needless to say, journeys like this trace a long and winding road. I had sent out packages before and received no response. I was leery. I found time to watch an NBA game between the Boston Celtics and the Philadelphia 76ers. The whole time I pondered how to motivate Solms. I went back and forth about the best tactic. I decided to forget sending a package. Instead I'd just show up the next day in his Philadelphia office. Then I figured I'd better tell him I was coming. I didn't want him to think me impulsive. An instant later, I got worried. What if he said, "hey, don't come"?

Providence smiled. Solms's grinning face and red shoes appeared in front of me on the tube. There he stood, on the edge of the basketball court, exhorting the Sunday afternoon 76ers crowd. The decision was made for me. He was not at home. In those days, nobody had cell phones. I couldn't call him. I hopped on a plane and was sitting outside his office as it opened the next day. We had a terrific meeting, the kind that makes you think the challenges are all worthwhile. I left exuberant. We had no final deal, but, he gave me a $150,000 check for an exclusive period in which to conduct due diligence. All I could say to myself was: *We were saved!*

Only we weren't. Welcome to real estate. We didn't do the deal with Solms. He backed out. And we were back to square one. Ironically, the solution came from a small bank, First National Bank of Jefferson (FNJ). FNJ had financed the $4 million in improvements made to the building for the Fair. Our failing to repay the bank loan would place the FNJ in serious jeopardy. In real estate parlance, "the bank was in the deal." FNJ had the same stakes we did. They needed us to succeed. We needed an additional $10 million to complete the apartment renovation.

FNJ went to its parent, Allied Bank of Dallas. Allied was a hero. It stepped in and completed the debt financing. During that period, businessman Jerry Derks brought in Merrill Lynch as an investor for the necessary equity investment. While great news, it brought other complications. The brokerage firm investment was contingent on the benefits of the federal historic tax credit. Unfortunately, these credits became much less valuable unless used prior to the end of year in which Merrill Lynch invested. Delivery of the credits required completion of the building. To do so, we had to finish a fifteen-month construction project in six months.

HRI could not afford outside architects or contractors, so we used our in-house team. Architect John Schackai, a lone practitioner, and Bill Doyle, an individual with construction experience, managed the design-build process. We felt positive about how things were going. Construction started in July 1985. Completion had to occur by year's end, but we were off to a good start.

Finally I was feeling comfortable. Heeding the advice of Monsignor Reynolds of St. Patrick's Church, in the early fall, I went to the Manresa retreat house. Located upriver from New Orleans, the plantation buildings situated along the Mississippi among grassy green fields and leafy oaks were an ideal place to reflect and meditate. There you are divorced from all communication. After the opening night dinner, you do not talk.

It was a stormy weekend. Still, I was feeling optimistic as I drove home on the I-10 towards New Orleans. But as I crossed the Bonnet Carré spillway, alarm bells went off in my head. I noticed that the lake was lapping up to the underside of the causeway. To say that was not ordinary was an understatement.

I turned on the radio and learned that an unseasonable hurricane had struck

Atrium of the Woodward Wight building, New Orleans, La.

New Orleans. After a heavenly weekend, I was returning to hell-week. Our workers, many from Mississippi, could not get to the job site. The hurricane did us no favors. Hitting a city once was bad enough. This damn thing turned around twice and as a result struck the city three times.

The tax credit delivery schedule, however, did not give time-outs for problems that Mother Nature causes. We had to complete by year's end. We threw ourselves into the project heart and soul. I stress this: our work force was *inspired*. They went full blast, giving us 24/7. They got it done. We filled up the building and obtained the rents needed. Fibre Mills was a success. And we were launched.

WOODWARD WIGHT

Our next project was the Woodward Wight building. The year was 1986. Ed had already bought this property. This would be the first mixed income residential project in Louisiana. Besides social importance, making it mixed income gave us access to bond financing. That enabled us to obtain a tax-exempt interest rate, lowered financing costs, and made the project financially feasible. Then, par for the course, came the blindside—President Ronald Reagan had pushed legislation that would make our bond financing impossible.

Senator Russell Long, then ranking Democratic member of the Senate Finance Committee, rode to the rescue. Long never hesitated to champion Louisiana. Notably, he deserves a lot of credit for bringing the Saints here, and he had ensured that WWL-TV, owned by the Roman Catholic Church, remained financially viable. A populist, Long recognized the value of mixed-income housing. He put a proviso into Reagan's tax legislation that exempted our project from its draconian restrictions on bond financing. True statesman, Russell Long.

Woodward Wight was a success. Since then, we've traveled a long way, always keeping our eye fixed firmly over the horizon. I'm proud of what HRI has become. The leadership of Tom Leonhard as President and Eddie Boettner as CAO and Co-Chair have created a talented, in-depth organization.

Tom's knowledge, energy, and exceptional feel for what makes a real estate deal financially viable for the company and investors ranks him among the savviest real estate executives anywhere. Eddie was a tremendous success as an entrepreneur at the time he joined HRI. He's built upon it as a tough-minded operating officer. He maintains discipline in a large organization that is distinguished by its esprit.

WHAT I REALLY LOVE ABOUT HRI
by Pres Kabacoff

What brought me to HRI was a belief that historic buildings, with big windows, high ceilings, St. Jo brick, and pine floors, located near the city center, would make the most attractive apartments in New Orleans. There was no comparison. I was excited about playing a role in taking a neighborhood in despair—the warehouse district—and bringing it back to life.

As HRI progressed, I felt we were on course for a broader mission. Our company had the ability to lead the revitalization of older cities. That became our stated mission. We define that as: *revitalizing cities by creating diverse, vibrant, and sustainable communities.* That sets us apart from the traditional developer. We're in business to make a profit. But I'm proud that our goals were broader. Ironically, businesses that focus solely on profits and growth do less well than those with inspiring visions. My co-founder, the late Edward B. Boettner felt the same way. He would be extremely pleased that HRI is flourishing in its efforts to—using his words— "revitalize cities all across America."

I love that HRI has built a team that has mastered the complexity of inner city revitalization. And it *is* complex. Mastering this complexity was hard earned. Today HRI offers a competitive advantage that allows us to deliver trophy real estate that provides extraordinary returns to our investors.

I love that HRI has been honored the Best Place to work in the City of New Orleans for our Corporate Headquarters.

I love that HRI has overcome the pejorative image that many developers carry. They bring that on themselves by putting profits above good design and community needs. Yes, taking on projects that transform a city incite controversy. Some throw stones for building too few or too many units of affordable housing. Others object that any neighborhood improvement makes it more costly to live here. Criticism goes with the territory.

Yet I love making the case to the critics that I have done my homework and that our projects employ absolute best practices in place making—walkable communities that are good for residents of all income levels and the environment. In HRI's headquarters city, one economist has reported our projects have created a $19 billion positive impact on the State and City's General Fund. I'm pleased that most civic and business leaders in the communities in which HRI has worked recognize what HRI has achieved. And I'm proud of it.

I love my civic work. Revitalizing cities takes more than bricks and mortar. It requires improving quality of life. A healthy city needs to be safe, well educated, provide good health, and be protected from environmental threats.

I love that I've had the opportunity to serve as a local and national leader on historic renovation and place based development. So civically I have focused on those issues.

HRI benefits from these civic activities. HRI works with governments and cities. If they recognize that you care about a city's prosperity and bettering the lives of its residents, you're going to thrive. Indeed, this sensibility animates the new generation known as "millennials." Deloitte Global's CEO recently observed that while millennials "believe the pursuit of profit is important to sustaining a business, [they] also say that pursuit must be accompanied by a sense of purpose, by efforts to create innovative products or services and, above all, by consideration of individuals as employees and members of society."

I have been long concerned about the devastating impact that concentrated poverty has on the life of a city. That led to HRI's selection to lead the revitalization of large public housing projects. This work has earned profits for the company while affording new opportunities for housing development residents. Our work with the State of Louisiana to forge a plan to finance housing after Katrina yielded federal gap financing for many HRI projects.

One issue that draws my focus is mass incarceration. In Washington and in state government, it is arguably the single issue that has caused parties to put partisan politics aside. It has united liberals like Nancy Pelosi and conservatives like Newt Gingrich. Our business partners, investors, and lenders appreciate that HRI shows community leadership. This quality is one of the things that make us interesting and attractive to these parties.

HRI is a progressive and caring company and I love that. All the things I love about the company and make it special and unique are what will attract national investors and allow HRI to be built to last.

The Developments

Courtyard of the Redemptorist Elderly Apartments.

Redemptorist Apartments

New Orleans, La. 1990

HISTORY

During the nineteenth century, today's Irish Channel was home to working class German and Italian immigrants, native Americans, and what the New Historic Landmark Commission terms "free people of color."[14] The channel derived its name from the flood of Irish fleeing the potato famine who arrived and resided in the area. Residents established a respectable neighborhood and became the city's laborers. Prior to the Civil War, the Irish dug the New Basin Canal that ran from Uptown to Lake Pontchartrain, clearing a swampy marshland. The work was difficult and risky. Indeed, slave owners declined to risk their labor on the project. The Irish stepped up and got the job done, although at a stiff price. As many as thirty thousand contracted yellow fever and perished.[15]

The survivors settled in the channel and worked on the bustling waterfront.[16] In 1833, the channel was incorporated into the City of Lafayette, distinguished by its townhouses and center hall cottages. In 1852, New Orleans's Anglo population struck up a political alliance with German and Irish immigrants, resulting in the annexation of Lafayette into the city of New Orleans.

Important jazz musicians of German, French, Irish, and Italian descent called the Irish Channel home, including Nick LaRocca and his Original Dixieland Jazz Band, celebrated as the first jazz band to record a phonograph record.[17] The diverse ethnic population drew the interest of the Catholic Church. It built three separate churches to serve different ethnic groups.

A complex of buildings occupied what became known as "Ecclesiastical Square." This included an orphanage, nine school buildings, a gymnasium, three churches, a priests' residence and gardens, two convents, stables, a laundry, and other supporting buildings.[18] The cornerstone of St. Mary's Assumption Church, built for speakers of the German language, was laid April 25, 1858.[19] That same day, St. Alphonsus, serving English speakers and drawing an Irish congregation, was consecrated across the street.[20] Redemptorist priests encouraged the French families to worship at Notre Dame de Bon Secours (Our Lady of Prompt Succor). St. Mary's achieved distinction partly through the leadership of Father Francis Xavier Seelos, who preached there until he fell victim in 1867 to yellow fever.

In 1918, a hurricane damaged Notre Dame, and the archdiocese consolidated all three churches into one parish. In 1925, it demolished Notre Dame. St. Mary's also suffered damage in 1965 when Hurricane Betsy struck but was restored through wide community support.

Redemptorist High School stood apart as the city's only coeducational Catholic school. It became famous for its marching band—a colorful feature of Mardi Gras parades—and a tough football team. Declining enrollment forced its closure in 1980.[21] The faculty and students moved to Gentilly and became Redeemer High School. In a cruel twist of fate, Redeemer closed after Hurricane Katrina flooded it with twelve feet of water.

The original Redemptorist complex consisted of five buildings: Liguori Hall, a masonry school building built in 1923 that contained the school auditorium;

Ecclesiastical Square, the heart of the New Orleans Irish Channel, circa 1900.

Redeemer Hall, a masonry school building opened in 1922; Selos Hall, an Italianate-style brick building whose construction commenced in 1867; the rectory, built around 1870 to serve St. Mary's Assumption and St. Alphonsus churches located across the street from Redemptorist; and a former convent, built in 1920 for the School Sisters of Notre Dame nuns.

REALIZING THE VISION

By the 1980s, the buildings, rectory, auditorium, convent, and three schools that made up the Redemptorist Complex had fallen into ruin. HRI saw the opportunity to create affordable housing for low-income elderly persons and provide a catalyst for neighborhood vibrancy. It developed a project to rehabilitate the structures.

The HRI renovation created 107 rent-subsidized one and two-bedroom apartments as the Redemptorist Apartments for low-income residents age sixty-two and older. These occupy three former school buildings and two former homes for priests and nuns.

When it opened in 1990, HRI co-founder Ed Boettner explained HRI's vision: "To the original developers of these buildings, Irish and German immigrants, the buildings represented hope for a better way of life. Our goal was to bring this same inspiration back into the Irish Channel neighborhood." Mayor Sidney J. Barthelemy underscored the point. "For many of the elderly moving in," he said, "this will be their first winter with adequate heat and housing." Beyond that, the project "is the first step to rebuilding a positive community in the Irish Channel."[22]

The project was a joint effort of the Archdiocese of New Orleans, the Housing Authority of New Orleans (HANO), the federal government, and HRI. HANO pays part of the rent, tenants pay the rest. Units have a full kitchen, private bath, central air conditioning and heat, and twenty-four-hour security. Grouped around St. Mary's Assumption Church, they have access to a 22,000 square-foot courtyard.

In 2005, Hurricane Katrina and vandals caused $15 million in damage to the property. In 2008, HRI renovated for the second time the historic chapel that formed a part of the development and repaired a statue of Christ that had stood in the main courtyard. Preservation Resource Center President Patty Gay praised the project effusively as "a perfect example of adaptive use of historic buildings."[23] HRI wanted to provide a special home for elderly citizens in need of affordable housing. Redemptorist is the incarnation of that vision.

Redemptorist forms a part of the lower Garden District that adjoined the St. Thomas Housing Project on one side and the classic Greek Revival homes on the other. St. Thomas had caused flight from the neighborhood, which had gone downhill. The revitalization of this storied complex redeemed an important element of the city's architectural and cultural history.

A revitalized Magazine Street, New Orleans, La.

Redeemer Hall, part of the old Redeptorist High School, circa 1955.

St. Mary's Assumption Church.

Redemptorist Elderly Apartments with the adjacent St. Alphonsus Church at right.

REDEMPTORIST
ELDERLY
APARTMENTS
AUTOMATIC
CAUTION
DOOR

PRIVATE PROPERTY
NO TRESPASSING

Main entrance of the Flint-Goodridge Apartments.

FLINT-GOODRIDGE

New Orleans, La. **1990**

Flint-Goodridge stood amid the Magnolia Housing Projects—officially C.J. Peete, named after its long-time manager, who served between 1952 and 1978. Known together as "Da Magnolia," the most distinguishing feature of the neighborhood was arguably the Brown Derby Bar, which served up strong drinks and provided a lively touch for its African American patrons. Located in Central City, the area deteriorated in the late twentieth century. Magnolia was viewed as notoriously dangerous. Yet its cultural contributions were significant.

New Orleans housing projects launched Bounce Music—a lively style of New Orleans hip hop that originated in the 1980s—and New Orleans Rap. According to journalist Sara Bonisteel, DJ Kenneth Williams, known as DJ Chicken, declared that "those two [beats] together make up dat beat."[24] Magnolia was home to many famous musicians. Birdman, Magnolia Shorty, Juvenile and Turk of the Hot Boys, and the rapper Jay Ellectronica got their start there.[25] The hugely successful Cash Money Records originated there and went on to ink a landmark distribution deal with Universal Music. Q93.3FM DJ Wild Wayne reminded Hot Boys star Lil Wayne of the days when he rang up the label to draw the notice of its co-founded Bryan "Baby Williams" by rhyming into the answering machine.[26]

Magnolia was the scene of Juvenile's hit song "Nolia Clap," inspired by the projects. Nearby on La Salle stands A.L. Davis Park, where brass bands have long paraded and Mardi Gras Indian tribes gather.[27] Great composers and musicians like Professor Longhair and Papa Celestin mention the park under its original name, Shakspeare Park (commemorating New Orleans mayor Joseph A. Shakspeare).

At this crossroads of cultural currents stood Flint-Goodridge Hospital. A legendary bastion of medicine, Flint-Goodridge was historically a beacon of hope for good health in an era in which too many people in the city lacked access to medical care. It closed in 1983. Over a decade later, HRI acquired and renovated the historic building into eighty-nine apartment units for elderly residents. Circumstances forced HRI to renovate it twice—before and after Katrina. HRI's work produced a landmark that has revitalized a core aspect of the city's tradition of caring as well as the surrounding neighborhoods.

HISTORY

The Flint-Goodridge Hospital evolved out of an urgent need to provide internships for African American medical students at New Orleans University. The university's first class graduated in 1892.[28]

Flint-Goodridge Hospital itself began in 1896 as the Phyllis Wheatley Sanitarium and Training School for Negro Nurses. The school was named after its founders, a small group of African American women known as the Phyllis Wheatley Club. In 1901, financial need forced the hospital to merge with New Orleans University's Medical College Hospital.[29]

The hospital was renamed Sarah Goodridge Hospital and Nurse Training School in honor of the mother of hospital benefactor Caroline Medge of Boston. That same year, the Medical College became Flint Medical College in honor of philanthropist John D. Flint, who had donated the money used to purchase the property on which the hospital was situated. In 1915, the hospital was renamed again, this time as Flint-Goodridge Hospital.[30]

During the 1930s, New Orleans University merged first with Straight College

Rear-view of Flint-Goodridge Hospital shortly after its opening in 1932.

The Dew Drop Inn, landmark musical venue and anchor of the Magnolia neighborhood.

and then into the new Dillard University. In 1932, the University moved the hospital into a new building located on Louisiana Avenue designed by architect Moise Goldstein in the "Fine Moderne" style.[31]

As its first superintendent, the Board selected Albert Walker Dent, a twenty-seven-year-old Atlanta native and Morehouse alumnus.[32] Dent's leadership forged the institution, Dillard President Dr. Samuel Dubois Cook observed, into "one of the four or five great historic black hospitals in the country."[33]

Because of segregation laws, the hospital provided African American doctors their only place to practice.[34] Indeed, it served as the only private hospital in New Orleans that admitted African Americans under the care of their own physicians. The city's first three African American mayors were born in this hospital.[35]

The hospital gained national fame as the "penny-a-day" hospital after *The Saturday Evening Post* described its innovative insurance plan, devised by Dent. [36] For a penny a day, members of the city's African American population could receive twenty-one days of hospitalization annually.[37] At first, the Board refused to embrace the program. Dent overcame objections when the Rosenwald Fund provided a $4,500 financial guarantee for the program. The Board's worries proved to be misplaced; Dent's plan was a resounding success, enrolling thousands of patients within a year. Dent was later named Dillard's third president and served with distinction for nearly three decades.[38]

In 1983, new financial challenges forced Dillard to close the hospital. Later that same year the property was sold to National Medical Enterprises, but the sale failed to revitalize the facility. The building stood vacant until 1989, when it was sold to HRI. It was at this time that HRI expanded its renovation capacity to provide housing for elderly low-income residents. Financing was complex. It required historic tax credits with Moderate Rehab credits that were available for affordable housing.

The major challenge lay in obtaining a 10 percent bump in financing from the U.S. Department of Housing and Urban Development (HUD) for what it termed "difficult-to-develop projects." To get in the door, HRI asked its non-profit co-sponsor, Christopher Homes, for support. Christopher Homes—an organization, not an individual—is the housing arm of the Catholic Church in New Orleans. HRI employee Billy Connick had once worked with Archbishop Philip Hannan and knew he was a strong supporter of elderly housing.

The Archbishop believed that if HUD's leadership could see what HRI intended, support would come. Congresswoman Lindy Boggs agreed and invited the new HUD Secretary, Jack Kemp, to be her guest at the Super Bowl being held in the city. A former All-Star American Football League quarterback for the San Diego Chargers and the Buffalo Bills, he gladly accepted and flew down for the event. Kemp made time to give HRI's project a close look. He liked what he saw and approved the 10 percent request.

Jack Kemp came to the original ground-breaking to help dedicate the apartments. Kemp extolled the project, declaring: "I would like to try and make these types of models come true in other cities around the country because you have really done something spectacular." *The Preservation News* proclaimed the Flint-Goodridge Apartments "a new symbol of hope for the city's poor" that demonstrates "the strength of rehabilitation efforts made possible through HUD."[39]

REALIZING THE VISION

The initial $5.5 million HRI project capitalized on a structure that was rich with a history of medical care and professional development. HRI renovated the exterior façade and repaired the stucco and brick. It preserved the original historic doors and windows. Existing trees were preserved, while new landscaping and sidewalks created a park-like atmosphere for social engagement. The renovated building features ornamental parapet wall reliefs, vertical brick ribs that separate window bays, and a central bay that defines the building entrance.

Hurricane Katrina inflicted extensive damage. Flooding poured ten feet of

Front-view of Flint-Goodridge Hospital facing Louisiana Avenue shortly after its opening in 1932.

Two views of the redeveloped Magnolia Housing Project.

water into basement units while the wind ripped away edges of the roof. In addition, looters stole copper wiring from air-conditioning compressors and refrigerant lines, causing water to gush and damage the upper floors that had remained dry. Plumbing and HVAC equipment were also stolen.

The second restoration thus faced formidable obstacles. "The building was begging to be fixed up," says HRI Development Project Manager Chris Clement. "Because it was an old building, the bones were strong. It was very fixable. But renovations required a lot of resources, especially after Katrina." HRI surmounted those obstacles through federal low-income housing tax credits (all Flint-Goodridge apartments are affordable to low-income elderly). Federal and state historic tax credits for restoration were awarded as HRI worked closely with the National Park Service to restore the exterior masonry work and windows, and to repair original light fixtures and brickwork.

VIBRANCY RESTORED

The restoration completed, HRI moved to contact former residents. Many had spread across the country during and after Katrina. But the effort paid off. "Katrina turned lives head over heels. It was a relief for many to return home," Clement says. Today's warm community atmosphere, he adds, "is apparent everywhere you turn. Wonderful smells of comfort cooking waft through the hallways as senior residents stroll the perimeter of the community for exercise. There's almost a competition among residents to see who can offer visitors the most delicious hospitality. If you take a cookie from one resident, you had better take a cup of gumbo from another."

"Some of our residents delivered children in this hospital," says property manager Debbie Finley.[40] That acute historical sensibility infuses the community with an intimacy and personal bond that transcends the bricks and mortar. The results speak for themselves. Flint-Goodridge has helped attract new shops and restaurants to nearby Freret Street, and the neighborhood is flourishing.

REVITALIZING A NEIGHBORHOOD

Katrina laid waste not only to Flint-Goodridge Apartments but the surrounding neighborhood. HRI's first renovation had helped spur rejuvenation in 1989. The second renovation, after Katrina, breathed even more life into the area.[41] Fueled by strong support from city officials like Council Member Stacy Head, the Freret Street Corridor that runs downtown towards the apartments has come alive as a chic place for restaurants, nightclubs, and cafes. The decayed buildings of the Magnolia projects now consist of rows of freshly painted town homes with ornate balconies and manicured lawns. At stoops where drug dealers once sold dope and shot at rivals, reports journalist Rick Jervis, there is a clubhouse with a flat-screen TV and a pool for neighborhood kids.[42]

Side entrance of the Flint-Goodridge Apartments.

GERTIE BERNARD
Flint Goodridge Resident

"I was born at Charity Hospital," Bernard recounts, but "came from a small town called Reserve." She grew up there and attended Our Lady of Grace Catholic School in St. John Parish. Afterwards, she moved to New Orleans. Her first job was working at the famous Woolworth's department store on Canal Street, where she worked for eleven years. From there, she went to Dominican College, a college for female students, working in food service.

Eventually she wound up with a job at the historic Roosevelt Hotel—named for Teddy Roosevelt—where she worked in banquets. She came to Flint-Goodridge after a friend told her about it. She applied, and six months later was accepted as a resident. That was before Katrina. She went back to Reserve until the storm passed, then returned to Flint-Goodridge after it was renovated for the second time.

"I love the place. I feel like it is my home away from my home. The people are like relatives. I know a lot of the residents. They're all friends. It is a caring place. We take care of one another. I visit a lot of ladies everyday. People may die but you're always making new friends. People just look out for each other. When somebody gets sick, people pitch in around the clock. You never feel alone. Never feel like help is far away."

Across the street stands Harmony Oaks, which replaced the Magnolia Housing Development. "Harmony Oaks, which is a multi-family development, has made the whole community so beautiful. So has Liberty Place, which is on Toledano at South Liberty Streets. The neighborhood is really much nicer, much safer. The Ya Ya Art Center has just opened to empower creative youth. It opened this year and it's right across the street from Flint-Goodridge."

She likes the way the building is run. "The managers make all the difference. If there's a problem, even just misplacing something like keys, they're only too happy to roll up their sleeves and take care of it." She loves the fact that it's close to St. Charles. "You can always get a streetcar. My church is right there. We're right by the bus stop, in front of the building. So I can get to my doctors."

Lots of new stores and amenities have come into the neighborhood: Subway, Taco Bell, Michaels, PETCO, Ross, Raising Cane's restaurant, and Capitol One Bank. A blighted neighborhood has been revitalized, and Flint-Goodridge led the way. "I'm so happy there," she says.

EXIT

Rear-view of Flint-Goodridge Apartments.

DEBBIE FINLEY

Manager, Flint-Goodridge

Debbie is the czar who keeps the trains running on time in HRI apartment buildings and ensures that its passengers are happy and cheerful. She loves managing. "I've been in property management for twenty-five years but started with HRI Management in 2007. I'm a certified apartment manager through the Apartment Association of Greater New Orleans. I'm also a real estate agent.

"I think it's really my calling. I love helping people. I love making sure that the property is well kept and that the people have a wonderful place to live. It's been in my blood for a long time. Every time I see a blighted property, I say to myself: 'there's a place somebody can fix up so people can live in it.' I always want to help find good places for someone to live."

As a manager, she collects the rent and sees that services are handled. She's a problem solver. "That's the key to resident retention. I'm almost like a social worker. If people have a problem with rent, I find ways to get them resources so that they can make their rent and keep their apartment. Of course since I'm managing a business, you have to make sure that you stay within your budget. You keep costs down while finding resourceful ways to keep service going up."

She started off helping the elderly. More recently, she has moved into managing multi-family buildings. "That has its ups and downs but it's given me the opportunity to use my skills and my talents to help others in need. Some tenants don't read. I found resources to help them learn. We had [a] non-profit that started a GED program for people who did not finish high school. When Katrina damaged the senior citizens community at Hollygrove Senior Center, we made our community at Cypress available for them to use."

She reveres her tenants. "I was always touched by the consideration of Felma Lewis. She always prayed for me. If she saw me working in the office late, she'd show up in her scooter with a plate of food in her lap for me. Just to know that she cared about me that much made a lasting impression on me forever. She was always like that. She considered me family. Recently she passed on, but her published obituary had pictures of the two of us together. I was deeply touched."

All her residents make her feel a part of their family. "I'm invited to weddings, birthdays, family functions. I try to participate in everything I'm invited to. It makes me feel like, wow, I've brought something to their lives."

She's highly conscious of the historic role that Flint-Goodridge has played in the city's history. "I was excited to be a part of this. It was the first black hospital in New Orleans. We've had three mayors born in that hospital. When people talk about it, they still think of it as a hospital. People were born there. People died there. Now people live here. It is a wonderful home for independent living. I'm very proud to be its property manager. We won an award for it when I came aboard. That's one of the highlights of my career. God could have chosen anyone to manage this property. He chose me. I felt truly blessed.

"At Flint-Goodridge," she says, "we've revitalized the surrounding community. That's what I love about HRI. It makes a difference in people's lives. That's our mission. We give new life to old places."

Main entrance of the Bakery Condominiums.

THE BAKERY CONDOMINIUMS

New Orleans, La. **1992**

HISTORY

The National Biscuit Company was a forerunner to Nabisco and famous for turning out tins of Yellow Boy soda crackers. Large ferris-wheel devices carried trays around in the ovens, from which workers plucked the finished crackers and replaced them with new pans.

For HRI, the Bakery represented a logical follow up to its revitalization of the Fibre Mills and the Woodward Wight buildings to residential lofts. It was located across the street from Fibre Mills. Developing the Bakery did not qualify as pioneering. The success of the other two projects had demonstrated that a market existed for the Warehouse District.

THE CHALLENGE

One challenge in revitalizing this building lay in its unique distinguishing feature—the three large ovens for baking the crackers. Figuring out how to convert them into usable space for residential living required imagination. HRI's team found a way to surmount this challenge, and used the ovens as an integral part of the living space.

Redeveloping historic properties is not for the faint of heart. Each development presents unexpected obstacles. As construction commenced, HRI discovered an underground tank filled with pollutants. The state Department of Environmental Quality required HRI to clean up the site before construction could take place. HRI conducted substantial testing to show that the tank had no leaks that had contaminated the soil beneath the building. "It was a scary moment," recalls Tom Leonhard. "Had that occurred, the high cost of remediation might well have made the project financially unfeasible.

"We breathed a huge sigh of relief," Leonhard says. "We removed the tank, made certain the soil was clean, and DEQ allowed HRI to proceed."

REALIZING THE VISION

Alex Dipp of HRI Architects and Rudy Lightwell of Concordia Architects led the design team. The 80,000 square foot building was distinguished by the three free-standing brick ovens on the third and fourth floors. Each was twenty-seven feet tall and eighteen feet square. HRI kept them intact and converted them into separate apartments, two-stories each, with tall windows facing the street. Spiral stairways lead to light-filled second floors of these apartments. The roof above the ovens is lined with windows.

The apartments feature sixteen-foot ceilings, floor-length windows, and the bakery's original hard-rock maple floors. An atrium fills the center of the building, and features landscaping, a fountain, and art by resident Kate Sidwell. A separate two-story building contains additional apartments with a gathering area and rooftop pool.

Atrium entrance to the Bakery.

National Biscuit Company Building, AKA "the Bakery," circa 1940.

DIANNE WILSON
Resident, 927 Poeyfarre

Dianne Wilson's roots run deep in New Orleans soil. Her family's presence dates back to the late 1700s. She was educated at Southern University, where she studied sociology. She left in 1972 for Chicago, where her dad lived after her parents divorced. Her first job was with Household Finance, working as an assistant manager. When her mother was diagnosed with cancer in 1988, she returned home to take care of her.

Back in the city, she worked with Human Resource Student Employment at Tulane, then moved over to Loyola in Admissions. She also worked with WWL-TV as a collections coordinator in its advertising department. She had been living on the West Bank, but her experience in Chicago made the idea of living in the inner city more attractive. "What brought me to 927 was that it was near where I was working and it was located in a historic neighborhood."

"Security ranks high in my priorities," she says. "In Chicago, I got mugged a couple of times. Trust me, when you've had a .38 caliber gun pointed at your stomach, you're not too enthusiastic about an encore performance. When you look somebody in the eye and you see that their eyes are dead, security goes to the top when you look for a place to live. One great thing about 927 Poyferre is the tight security."

"I love that it is convenient. It's an art area. You can walk to everything that matters. The staff is excellent. Cindy Vallejos, who handles leasing there, is a total professional. She pays attention to all the needs of her tenants. She doesn't hesitate. If my air conditioning breaks, she gets it fixed within hours. She relates very well to other people."

Wilson loves the fact that it is a modern property in a historic area. "I love the blend. You get the history but all the modern conveniences. That's a lot to say for that." She feels that the impact of its location is terrific. "St. Patrick's is three blocks away. Shopping at the Riverwalk is a snap. When the parades come at Mardi Gras, they come to you. You don't have to go to them. It's a hoot."

JEANETTE GRAY

Resident, 927 Poeyfarre

Gray is a native New Orleanian who grew up on the West Bank and has lived here all of her life, except for Katrina, when she went to Texas, California, and New Jersey. During that post-storm period, she followed the nomadic existence experienced by most of the city's population that had to flee the rising waters.

She attended Frederick Douglass School on Huey P. Long Avenue and Lincoln High School in Marrero. After school she married Sylvester Crawford. When they divorced, she married Howard Bailey, to whom she was married for thirty-five years. She is a seamstress but worked as a dietician and cook at the Guest House on Eighth Street in Harvey.

Katrina kept her away from New Orleans for four years until she returned in 2009. "My grandmother told me about an apartment building in the Warehouse District. I put in an application and was accepted." She loves living there. "I'm a diabetic and a cancer survivor. I didn't have transportation and 927 is accessible to bus routes. My doctors are all on the West Bank. It's such an easy walk to Convention Boulevard to catch a bus to go see them. It's so convenient."

She treasures the privacy of 927. "Nobody can get to me. I'm safe. I'm happy. I love the people. They're so great. I'm on the fourth floor. People have come and gone, but everybody is cordial and polite. You meet people from other floors. There's a friendly conversation. I go in the patio. It's lovely. Our maintenance guy, Paul, is there. Always helpful."

The building comes especially alive during holidays, particularly Thanksgiving and Christmas. "We have 'floor picnics,' full of gaiety and laughter. Everybody brings something. It's a very nice atmosphere." She has a lot of younger friends. They love to tease. And they're caring. "It's the kindnesses that you remember the most. Once I felt unwell in the elevator. People who came in saw that, and watched me until I got in my door." She likes the fact that the residents hail from different age brackets. "It keeps us all young," she smiles.

Another thing that strikes her is that 927 is pet friendly. "We have large pets and small ones. Yet people keep their pets under control. The pets contribute to the warm atmosphere that makes living easier." She loves the location. "I love that I can look out my window and see the city. I'm not in the heart of it, but it's right there if I want to be there. Restaurants are around us. There's a lot of calm activity, a lot of people going about their lives, and you never feel isolated. People in our building love to talk about the Saints. If I say Saints and somebody is willing to listen, we've got a conversation."

She appreciates the high standards of maintenance. "It's simply a homelike atmosphere. During Katrina, we lost everything. Here I feel as if I've received it all back."

Main entrance of the the Cotton Mill residential development.

THE COTTON MILL

New Orleans, La. 1998

HISTORY

Eli Whitney's invention of the cotton gin in 1793 made cotton king in the South. The machine separated cotton fibers from the seeds, a job previously done by hand. By 1826, it had replaced sugar and rice as New Orleans's biggest export. By the outbreak of the Civil War, southern states provided two-thirds of the world's supply of cotton. The growth of this industry paralleled the growth in slavery, which increased from 700,000 slaves in 1790 to over 3 million in 1850. The increase in slaves was an important cause of the Civil War.[43]

Much of the cotton grown in the South was shipped through the busy port of New Orleans to New York, and from there, on to Britain. Later, cotton was processed on the docks of New Orleans and shipped directly to England. After the Civil War, merchants established the Cotton Exchange to expand the city's prosperity. Edgar Degas, one of the towering figures in French Impressionism, painted his uncle's cotton factoring office in New Orleans in 1873.[44]

The port of New Orleans flourished, but the changes brought fateful consequences. Growing commercial demands for warehousing and manufacturing plants that supported the port displaced residential housing. Brick warehouses, factories, foundries, and cotton and sugar presses filled the area. At the turn of the century, these were succeeded by concrete buildings that supported other industries located in the metropolitan area.[45]

By the mid-twentieth century, the shift from handling cargo by stevedores to containers caused the port to move up and down river to new locations that could house containers. Abandoned and blighted, the once thriving commercial area became a center for the homeless, until the 1984 World's Fair led to the neighborhood's rejuvenation.

THE COTTON MILL

Constructed in 1882, the building that is now the Cotton Mill Apartments and Condominiums is the largest warehouse building in the Warehouse District. It sits on a piece of New Orleans that has a storied history. The land was once owned by the Jesuits. In 1765, Francois Duplessis acquired ownership and built a plantation home on the site of what is now Annunciation and Poeyfarre streets. A succession of French families owned the house, including the Fouchers, the Delord-Sarpys, and the Duplantiers. The plantation home—known as the old Duplessis house—stood until the Maginnis Cotton Mill was erected on the site around 1882. The mill employed Irish workers who turned raw cotton into fabric and rope.

During the mid-nineteenth century, the site also hosted the Fasnacht Brewery. Opened in 1852, the brewery continued through successive owners operating under mostly similar names, and went out of business in 1875. Seven years later Arthur Maginnis bought the brewery and the rest of the block and built upon it the world's largest cotton mill. Maginnis owned it until 1914, when he was convicted of tax fraud. The mill was sold but continued operating until 1944.[46]

In the 1990s, HRI acquired the property to renovate the buildings into elegant apartments and condos. Recognizing its historic importance, it underwrote an archeological dig led by University of New Orleans archeologist Shannon Dawdy. The dig turned up a wealth of historic fragments that dated to the eighteenth century: French wine bottle seals, an 1848 U.S. half-dime, French pottery, Civil War bullets. There were even play marbles, apparently dating from Madame Florian's Seminary for the Education of Young Ladies, established in 1810 on the larger plantation site to instruct pupils on "the Ornamental Accomplishments as well as those branches of Knowledge most useful to the female sex." Adjacent to the house until around 1832 was an amusement park, Eliza Gardens. Its operator, Luc Munge, declared "no person will be admitted without paying one bit at the door." Munge also made a point of stating that parents were responsible for the behavior of their children.[47]

Among those participating in the archaeological dig were Mandeville country club manager David Duplantier, who descended from one of the plantation's owners, American Revolutionary War veteran Armand Duplantier.[47] Armand was among those appointed to receive Gilbert du Motier, the Marquis de Lafayette, on his 1825 sojourn to New Orleans. "Very few times can you actually see family history," Duplantier told the *Times-Picayune*. "Usually you just kind of see names in books." Another descendant, Stephen Duplantier, recounted that Armand loved fine French wines as they evoked memories of his birthplace in a mountainous region of France.[49]

Dawdy views the site as a record that unveils the history of the Warehouse District as well as the Lower Garden District. "We developed a picture of how the city developed, from 1765 as a French rural plantation, to suburbanization, urbanization, and then a more industrial area," she said.[50]

SECURING APPROVALS

Renovating the Cotton Mill required concurrent approvals from local, state, and federal officials. An HRI team headed by Gary Meadows (architect), Tom V. Crumley (development project manager), Jackie Case-Redding (architectural project manager), and Rob Wooderson (construction project manager) presented applications, designs, architectural plans, and financial plans to relevant authorities.

The City of New Orleans reviewed plans to ensure that they met building and safety code requirements. The Historic Districts Landmark Commission and the Preservation Resource Center reviewed plans to ensure appropriate preservation of the buildings for adaptive reuse. HRI donated the façade to the Preservation Resource Center. At the state level, the State Historic Preservation Office gave its approval.

As the building is listed on the National Register of Historic Places and plans envisioned changes to the building exterior and to the courtyard, National Park Service approval was required. Its rules prohibit visually altering the structure in any significant way. HRI wanted to put new penthouse apartments on the roof. The Park Service objected on grounds that they were visible from the street. The HRI team built a full-scale model of the Cotton Mill, with the penthouses, and took it to Park Service headquarters in Washington. They set the model on top of a large conference table. Pres Kabacoff asked Park Services to get down on their knees and look up. "I promise, you won't see the addition," he advised. They did so, and from their hands and knees, looked up. The table simulated ground level, and the model the existing building with the new addition. Looking up from their kneeling position simulated the perspective of the person-on-the-street. The penthouses were not visible. The project was approved.

REALIZING THE VISION

Work began in October 1996 and was completed in April 1998. HRI transformed the Cotton Mill building into 269 apartments and seventeen penthouse units.[51] Design and architecture presented a sensitive challenge. This adaptive reuse transformed an industrial building into a residential use. HRI's goal was to provide fine living in a secure environment, while preserving the historic luster that made the Cotton Mill special.

The modern site included a complex of buildings. HRI gutted seven brick buildings that occupied the full block, bounded by Annunciation, Constance, Poeyfarre, and John Churchill Chase streets. The area between the buildings forms a 25,000-square-foot courtyard. It's ornamented with relics recovered from the textile mill as a reminder of its heritage. Indeed, "salvage art" sculptures forged by Paul Fowler who reused one hundred-year-old scraps of boilers, sprinklers, and electrical machinery, highlight different parts of the Cotton Mill. Many retain their dust coating. "The sculpture contributes to the ambience," project manager Tom Crumley said.

Crumley also noted that "retaining the aura of the past was central to the design and ethos. While carefully preserving the exteriors, we designed the interiors to create even in smaller units a sense of space. We retained exposed brick walls, old wooden columns and huge timber ceiling beams." The renovated buildings each contain wide corridors with fifteen-foot high ceilings, lined by units that face either to the courtyard or the city. Some corridors feature the original wooden columns spaced seven to eight feet apart. Mounted on metal plates, they are painted gray from the floor to a height of roughly six feet, and brown from there to the ceiling, reflecting the original color scheme. The ceilings are open, with cables, conduit, and air- conditioning ducts running the length and completely visible.

"We retained the brick surfaces as they were, many bearing splashes of paint," Kabacoff said. "They look as they did in the nineteenth century. We painted and patched where necessary in order to ensure structural integrity." While some floors are cement, others retain their original hardwood, sanded and coated with polyurethane.

Architect Gary Meadows recalls the enormity of the undertaking:

> It was a huge building with 300,000 square feet of building constructed in 1882. It had wonderful load bearing brick walls and timber structures. The most remarkable thing was the windows. They had operable cypress windows five feet wide and twelve feet tall. The National Park Service placed

Myles Salt Company, AKA "the Cotton Mill," circa 1940.

> a priority on the restoration and preservation of these 1,100 windows. HRI had its own construction company. One of my most wonderful memories was that inside the building during construction they built a window repair/assembly line, and using old, recycled cypress materials, did a careful and thoughtful restoration of the wood windows. It was marvelous to walk through there and watch all these carpenters working and repairing the windows. That proved the lynchpin to securing the historic tax credits on the project.[52]

The apartments feature tall ceilings ranging between twelve and twenty feet high, and windows five feet wide and twelve feet tall that fill the units with natural light. Achieving that was a vast undertaking. "There are 1,100 double-sash windows. We removed all 2,200 sashes, removed all lites, repaired or rebuilt all mutins, and reinstalled the lites and reglazed the windows. They even have the old counter-weights, enabling them to open and close easily."

Meadows notes that design presented a surprise: "We had no original drawings of the Cotton Mill. We had to go out and measure the building. We laid out 297 designed apartments within the building. We realized that the building was not square. It was about three degrees off on the grid. We had to adjust the layout to accommodate this unusual shape. It was an interesting layout challenge."

The biggest challenge resulted from the desire to create seventeen roof-top terrace new construction residential units that would maximize the beautiful views of New Orleans on one side and the Mississippi River on the other.

Midway through the process, there was a program change. Instead of using them as rental apartments, HRI had the opportunity to sell them as condominiums. Says Meadows: "We upgraded the finishes with a premium placed on views. We had always thought that the great view was of the downtown skyline. Once we got up on the roof, we realized that the view towards the river and uptown was splendid. We made a dramatic design change to each unit. We created a mezzanine level corridor below the rooftop level. That enabled us to provide access to each penthouse apartment from below, allowing both uptown and downtown views in each unit."

Apartments are furnished with modern appliances. There is a 1,500 square foot, well-equipped fitness center. Outside, the courtyard features a large swimming pool and a pergola that was fashioned from a brick wall that was left standing and welded steel mesh. One building contains a clubhouse. Nearby, a circular brick area, topped with cement, serves as an entertainment stage. Three distinctive features include the 140-foot water tower (which disguises a cellular telephone tower); a large, unchanged smokestack; and the three-sided clock tower.

VIBRANCY RESTORED

The project is an architectural gem. *Multi-Housing News Magazine* and the National Association of Home Builders Multifamily Council named it the best multifamily rehabilitation project in the nation. The Home Builders Group chose the project as the winner of its 1998 Pillars of the Industry Award, besting over three hundred competitive developments in that category.

The Cotton Mill draws high praise from residents. "All the beauty of old industrial architecture with modern amenities," wrote one on a yelp.com listing.[53] New restaurants, galleries, museums, markets, parks, and shops fill the nearby area within easy walking distance. The complex has a magnificent lobby that houses a concierge desk.[54]

The Cotton Mill exemplifies HRI's goal of sparking revitalization in historic areas. HRI helped pioneer that process in the New Orleans Warehouse District, giving it new life, with a view to the future that preserves the city's unique architectural heritage. Edward B. Boettner and Pres Kabacoff stood next to one another in the courtyard at the opening. Ed turned to his partner and declared: "We went way beyond our budget to create this masterpiece." Gazing at what they had achieved, Pres smiled. "Well, look at it this way. We created the most beautiful garden courtyard in the city of New Orleans."

COTTON
MILL

COTTON
MILL

Iberville Street façade of one of the former D.H. Holmes buildings.

D.H. Holmes

New Orleans, La. **1996**

HISTORY

D.H. Holmes was a New Orleans department store founded in 1842 by Daniel Henry Holmes. An Ohio native orphaned at age two and lacking any formal education, he became one of the nation's greatest success stories in retailing. He got his start when his neighbor Eugene Levassor hired him as his valet and taught him French and to play the lute. At age seventeen his uncle sent him to New York City to work for Lord & Taylor clothing store.

When Lord & Taylor decided to open a branch in New Orleans, it selected Holmes to head the enterprise, as French was the primary spoken language there.[55] The branch was a bold move, and it proved no great success. Holmes saw an opening for himself and purchased the failed store, reopening it in 1842 on Magazine Street as the Daniel Holmes Store. Shortly after, he moved it to more fashionable quarters on Chartres Street.[56]

In 1849 he shifted the store to Canal Street. At first he employed only men as clerks. When men left to fight in the Civil War, he hired women to take their places and retained them even after the war ended. The store prospered under Holmes's simple philosophy: "Give the best product and the best service for the lowest price." As service-minded as Holmes might have been, he was still a hard-nosed businessman; his store accepted only cash, no credit.[57]

Holmes based D.H. Holmes upon stores like Le Bon Marché in Paris. He purchased all of his merchandise in Europe, earning a reputation abroad as the "King of New Orleans."[58] Certainly the store justified his august reputation. Large storefront windows flanked the entrance and showcased elaborate displays that highlighted high fashion, elaborate scenes from Russian history, or fantasies that lent an air of glamour. The rear of the store featured a huge, ornately framed French mirror and became a gathering place for well-coifed and fashionably attired young ladies. The store consciously created an atmosphere of elegance that encouraged customers to wear their best outfits when they came to shop. Women were encouraged to wear their finest clothing when shopping. It was "white glove" shopping for a sophisticated clientele and the store's well-trained staff. Its storied cafeteria acquired distinction for its cuisine and as a place for socialites to convene.[59]

D.H. Holmes was more than a store. It was an *experience* and a *destination*. In today's era, one would compare it to New York's Bergdorf Goodman or Henri Bendel. While marketing a wide range of clothing and items, D.H. Holmes was ritzy.

The stories became their own legends. Well into the 1950s, one shopper recalled: "We would get dressed up and go shopping with my mom. We each got our pick of candy from the candy counter IF we had behaved ourselves. Of course I always got a huge chunk of white chocolate. Mmmmmmmm." Another declared that going to Holmes "was more of an event than just shopping. We could go to every department with my grandmother. You bought something from almost every department . . . boy, what great memories!!!" Another summed up the experience this way: "This store, like so many others gone now, just felt comfortably right and special as a part of our lives and social habits. Anyone who grew up here knows exactly what I mean."[60]

By the end of the nineteenth century it had grown into the largest department store in the South. Meeting under its clock on Canal Street became a storied point of rendezvous that gained legendary status in John Kennedy Toole's magnificent novel, *A Confederacy of Dunces*. As the story opens, the protagonist, Ignatius Reilly, is "looking for people dressed in bad taste" while waiting there to meet his mother.

By the 1980s, D.H. Holmes had eighteen stores and was a major independent retailer. In 1989, Dillard's Department Stores purchased the company, but then decided that downtown main street stores no longer worked. It closed the Canal Street store. As the last of the major retailers to close, this was a death-knell for Canal Street. Mayor Sidney Barthelemy asked them to donate the property to the city, and seeing a big tax deduction, Dillard's was happy to oblige.

THE PROPERTIES

The city sent out an RFP (request for proposals) to revitalize the D.H. Holmes buildings, and a competition developed. HRI proposed converting them into upscale hotel suites and apartments. Developer Shea Dixon offered to turn the main building into a Grammy Hall of Fame and Music Museum that would spotlight famous jazz, rock, pop, and other musicians. Bolstering his case, Dixon publicized two polls taken by Dr. Ed Renwick of Loyola University that both suggested strong public and business leader preference for Shea's idea.

The mayor decided that HRI's approach, which would shift Canal Street from large department stores to residential, hotel, and entertainment made the most sense. He also recognized that HRI could get the financing. Barthelemy relates, "the decision was not close. HRI was the clear choice."

REALIZING THE VISION

Having won the right to develop the project, HRI faced a significant obstacle in funding it. The national hotel financing market had run dry. HRI required nearly three years to secure financing. HRI's strategy lay in convincing local lenders that revitalizing Canal Street was vital to the city's future.

Major retail stores had gone out of business or exited to the suburbs, leaving the city's most important downtown shopping thoroughfare vacant and blighted. Kabacoff and Boettner argued bringing back this area would help the entire city. "The key," Kabacoff says, "was to show that while Maison Blanche, Holmes, Gus Mayer, F.W. Woolworths, Godchaux's, and other department stores were history, we could revitalize Canal Street with tourism, entertainment, and residential living. We also had to persuade the city to supplement private with public funding." That was an innovative approach. No prior project had truly been a public/private partnership. Kabacoff's idea for financing Holmes broke new ground.

Kabacoff turned to economist Tim Ryan. Ryan directed him to his brother, Ashton Ryan, then president of the original First National Bank of Commerce.[61] Ryan agreed to support the project if Kabacoff could recruit four other banks to join in a loan plus gain financial guarantees from the hotel operator. He succeeded. The Sonesta Corporation, which operated hotels, stepped up and guaranteed the loan. This was a sweet success for Pres Kabacoff. Twenty-five years earlier, Sonesta had done business with his father, Lester, to operate the Royal Orleans Hotel—the first new hotel to operate in the French Quarter in a hundred years. FNBC and Sonesta's decisions prompted three other local banks to join in the financing.

Canal Street façade of the former D.H. Holmes department store.

On the public side, the city created the Canal Street Development Corporation (CSDC)—city-owned—and designated it the landlord for the project. CSDC would function as a private party and lease the property. Board member Jose Canseco worked with Kabacoff, and CSDC facilitated a $1 million Urban Development Action Grant (UDAG) and a $5 million HUD 108 loan to the development. Chevron Corporation provided the equity derived from historic tax credits. It was their first hotel development investment.

THE DEVELOPMENT

Seventeen different parcels comprised the D.H. Holmes complex. The original D.H. Holmes building fronted on Canal Street. In 1964, Holmes had covered its 1913 façade facing this historic street with a modern one, but HRI restored its original neo-classic appearance. Redeveloped as a full-service hotel, the main building opened in 1995 at 800 Iberville Street as the Chateau Sonesta Hotel. In 2012, it underwent a major renovation and became the Hyatt French Quarter Hotel.[62]

The annex at 810 Bienville Street runs between Bienville and Iberville streets. Formerly serving as the adjacent warehouse to the department store, a bridge had once connected the two buildings. Zoning regulations located the annex within the French Quarter where construction of new hotels was prohibited, so HRI made the decision to convert the property into apartments. HRI demolished the connecting bridge and within the annex created eighty-seven luxury units as the D.H. Holmes Apartments. The recently updated apartments feature Mannington Wide Plank Wood Flooring, GE stainless steel appliances, vaulted ceilings in living spaces, a state-of-the-art fitness center, a rooftop deck with a boutique style swimming pool, and attached garage parking.[63]

The hotel and apartments are steps from some of the city's most glamorous restaurants as well as the world famous Bourbon Street. HRI President Tom Leonhard observed that "the buildings are part of New Orleans's history and they stand as proud reminders of it and the city's progress."

To commemorate *A Confederacy of Dunces* protagonist Ignatius Reilly, Kabacoff commissioned sculptor William Ludwig to create a full-body bronze cast of the character. Today it stands on Canal Street at the entrance to the hotel, beneath the renowned clock. While D.H. Holmes was a department store, people said, "Meet me under the clock." Thanks to HRI's renovation, they still do.

Bronze cast of Ignatius Reilly under the D.H. Holmes clock.

Entrance to the Hyatt French Quarter, part of the former D.H. Holmes complex of buildings.

Dauphine Street façade of one of the former D.H. Holmes buildings.

TRAVIS TAGUE

General Manager, Hyatt French Quarter Hotel

I was born and raised in Gretna, Louisiana. I graduated from the University of New Orleans in hotel, restaurant, and tourism. I've worked in the industry here in New Orleans for twenty years. I started out as a bus boy at Tony Mandina's, a local family-owned restaurant on the west side of the Mississippi, which as all of us born [here] know, is really the east side of the river. The spark created then is still what drives me. I want to create an experience for customers.

You wouldn't think a bus boy could do that, but you can. You learn what customers want, not just what they need. That translates to where I am today. As a general manager, I pay close attention to what guests and my staff want and need.

I started with HRI as an Area Director of Human Resources. I was attracted by the desire of the company to have a positive influence on the community and its neighborhoods. I had known a few people who had worked for HRI. They were enthusiastic. I joined [so I could] be on a team with similar people who brought a high level of energy and enthusiasm to work.

One thing that motivates me is developing the talents of my colleagues and staff. I received a letter from a staff person. He took the time to write by hand, in pencil, a three-page letter [on] loose-leaf paper. I was impressed that he had taken the time to do so. He thanked me for always standing up for the staff. No problem, he said, was too big or too small to warrant my assistance. He said that I had the ability to put the staff at ease and feel confident. I was touched and flattered.

The takeaway for me is, you never know who's watching. This fellow watched in the dish room. His letter registered the influence that just a single individual can have on others in the building through their actions. You can inspire, mentor, and energize through action. At the French Quarter Hyatt, we've created a culture that no matter the rank or title, everybody is on the same team. It's all about creating a good experience for guests and colleagues alike.

I'm still early in my career. I want to grow and develop. I want to help my colleagues do so. I want to improve physically, mentally, and spiritually. I will never settle for what today is. Tomorrow presents new challenges and new ambitions and new desires.

Night view of a revitalized Canal Street.

AMERICAN CAN COMPANY

AMERICAN CAN FACTORY

New Orleans, La. 2001

What was most striking about the neighborhood in which American Can Apartments stood was its eclectic nature. Part poor, part affluent—part of it was a park, part of it was a vacant industrial corridor with a railroad track running through it. Located two miles north of downtown, American Can itself stood vacant and blighted. A large property that dominated the landscape, its renovation signaled a Mid-City comeback.

HISTORY

At one time, the Tin Can Trust controlled a significant percentage of the American business in tin cans, containers, and packages of tin. During World War II, it played a major role in military production. Headquartered in Connecticut, the company owned the American Can Company manufacturing plant until it closed in 1988.[64]

The property is located on 6.3 acres of New Orleans in a formerly swampy area dotted with dairy farms and cemeteries that nineteenth-century residents called "Back of Town"—meaning, back of the natural levees along which the city had developed. Historian Edward Branley reports that the term referred originally to the streets and neighborhoods like Tremé that stood in the "back" of the French Quarter, while those facing the Mississippi River were known as the "front." Nationally renowned musician Troy "Trombone Shorty" Andrews hailed from the original back of town and named his second album Backatown. As the city expanded towards Lake Pontchartrain past Broad Street (the official boundary of Treme) the area took the name Mid-City, embracing neighborhoods from Faubourg St. John near City Park and extending to Gentilly. Streetcar and bus lines offered service known as Backatown lines.[65]

Until the arrival of Europeans, Native Americans lived on the higher ground that runs along Bayou St. John. By the mid-1830s the city had built the Carondelet and New Basin Canals, and in the 1890s a new pumping station was built at Broad and Bienville streets. But what made the area habitable was Albert Baldwin Wood's invention of the screw pump, which allowed water to be pumped from land that was below sea level. Wood's pump enabled the city to drain the mosquito-infested swamps, and by the early 1900s the area saw major development, with improved drainage, more homes, and new industry—including the American Can Company.[66]

One of the largest manufacturing plants in the South, the American Can complex (bounded by Orleans Avenue, North Genois, Toulouse, and North Cortez streets) included six buildings and associated facilities, including adjoining metal buildings, loading docks, and connecting rail lines. Constructed between 1907 and 1929 the plant is listed on the National Register of Historic Places. It stands a few blocks away from City Park, the largest green space in the city, and Bayou St. John. On one side stands a historic residential neighborhood, and by car, it is five minutes from the Central Business District. The surrounding neighborhood boasts diverse architectural styles that provide a colorful combination: shotgun cottages dating from the late 1800s with "gingerbread ornaments," bungalows, and Tudor and mission-style homes built in the 1920s. In the 1900s, the area had a large Hispanic population. And while today it still has the largest percentage of Hispanics in the city, a majority of the residents are African American.[67]

American Can Company began canning operations in 1906 and at one time had 1,500 employees. It ceased operation in 1987, leaving the building abandoned. Decay soon set in.

THE CHALLENGE

A fire damaged all but the outside walls of Building 6 of the complex, which was nearly demolished. This building was a ruin and filled with lead and asbestos. Fortunately, the two perimeter walls facing Toulouse Street and the north side of the site were intact. In a touch of irony, architect Gary Meadows retrieved a piece of history from the ashes of the fire. "On my first walk of the site," he recounts wryly, "I noticed a couple of 'heart pine' old timber beams that were not completely burned. I had those removed and refabricated into a new dining room table. The moral of the story is that out of that trash pile lay a two hundred-year-old tree that has been a wonderful addition to our family."

At left: the American Can Factory with Bayou St. John in foreground.

The project confronted different challenges. To secure approval from the city's Historic Districts and Landmarks Commission to preserve the buildings for residential living, HRI had to—and did—win support for its plan over competing suggestions to use the space for "big box" retail stores. HRI acquired the site and developed it into 265 one, two, and three bedroom apartments and nearly a dozen retail establishments in 444,000 square feet of space.

REALIZING THE VISION

Revitalizing this property presented obstacles. Says Meadows:

> The most interesting thing about this project was that HRI was able to make the project work when for 20 years every contractor and developer had taken a stab at converting it into a modern use and failed. One challenge was the size, over 400,000 square feet. But the larger challenge was that 80% of the walls consisted of windows that had to be refabricated, reworked and refurbished. We had to surmount problems of air conditioning, glazing the exterior of the façade and water-proofing. People don't realize that when you convert a non-air conditioned industrial business into one suited for living, the challenge is enormous. Industrial buildings can accept moisture inside the walls. That does not work for residential units. We had to make the building water-tight.

Many of the earlier design proposals for American Can that HRI reviewed created atriums in the center of the buildings to let light into them. "We saw a unique opportunity," Meadows says. "We did not create any interior atriums. We designed units that were larger than we might normally design for the market place and offset that [by] keeping the finishes minimalist. We had exposed concrete floors and ceilings. There were twenty-two-foot wide structural bays that contained bands of windows that could not be interrupted by partitions, leading to the more open loft designs."

Design architects elected to work with the brick and timber frame as well as new additions that employed a brick-on-concrete technique. The design incorporated the cement and longleaf pine pillars as a visual touch within apartments. In achieving that goal, units were designed around the pillars. Among the plant's most striking features were its 1,200 windows with bays that were eighteen feet long by ten feet high. The design maintained the building's distinctive color schemes, rooted in red brick, white trim and plasters, and green window frames that echoed the traditional New Orleans color for window shutters. The design team decreed that "only walls that had been originally painted be again painted, while other walls were left as they were. Signs that indicated exits and load limitations were kept as permanent references to American Can Company's industrial past."[68]

Designers were proud of the high ceilings and the success in blending the old and the new. Despite the large scale of the project, HRI created a sense of intimacy. "You get the loft idea," resident Nick Silvy observed, "but it doesn't feel as if you're living in a warehouse."[69]

The four story brick masonry walls with window opening that had survived the fire were retained as architectural features. The concrete pilasters were utilized as aesthetic features around a new courtyard swimming pool.

Tom Leonhard summed up the project this way: "We wanted to transform an old factory into a unique place to live, near City Park and near neighborhoods that needed revitalization. The project is a testament to the positive impact that adaptive reuse can achieve."

The vibrant Mid-City neighborhood along Bayou St. John, near the American Can Factory.

Main entrance of the American Can Factory residential development.

AMERICAN CAN
APARTMENTS

Orleans Avenue view of the American Can Factory residential development.

At Right: aerial view of the rear of the American Can Factory, including solar panels.

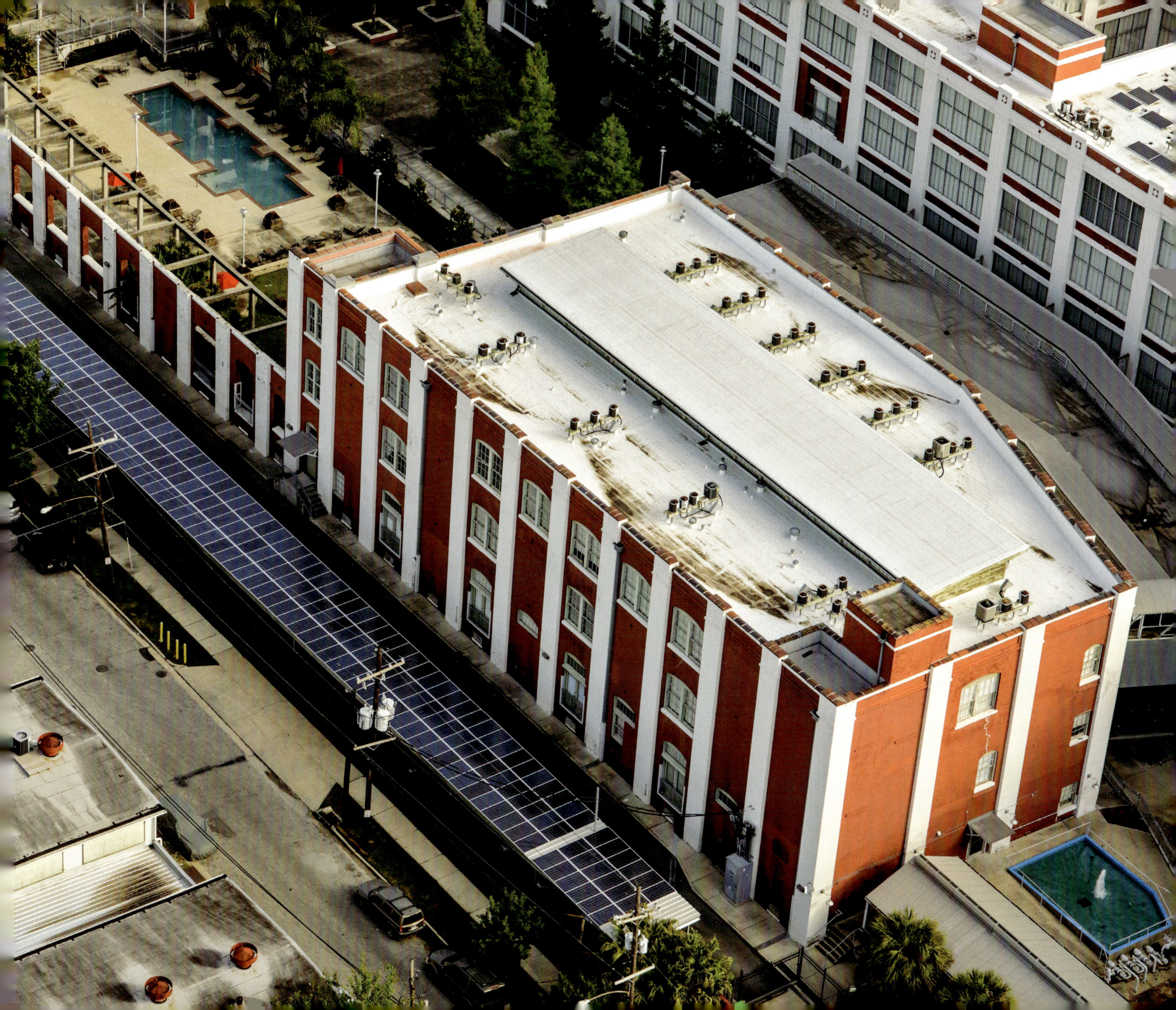

Renaissance Grand Hotel, St. Louis, Missouri.

RENAISSANCE GRAND HOTEL / MERCHANDISE MART

St. Louis, Mo. 2002-03

St. Louis is one of America's great cities. Yet by the 1990s, it had suffered the largest loss of inner city population among any U.S. city. Population in St. Louis County had declined from 900,000 to 350,000. Exquisite, historic buildings were abandoned and entire neighborhoods needed revitalization. Former New Orleans mayor Sidney Barthelmey had thought about St. Louis and saw opportunities to help restore life to a great city. Because the area was derelict, the key lay in forging public-private partnerships. Conventional financing would not work; the city had to provide a subsidy.

In his effort to support historic tax credits in Congress, Pres Kabacoff met with Missouri Congressman and Democratic Party Majority Leader Dick Gephardt, also a champion of the credits. Gephardt suggested that Pres Kabacoff visit St. Louis and related the invitation to Sidney Barthelemy. Now head of government relations for HRI, Barthelemy, who had served as President of the National League of Cities, knew St. Louis. While attending a conference of African American mayors in St. Louis, he met with the city's mayor, Clarence Harmon. Harmon was immediately interested and invited HRI to visit. Harmon convened a meeting in his offices attended by Barthelemy, Kabacoff, and the St. Louis preservation community leadership, including the president of the local historical society. They all agreed that the city's historic buildings needed a new lease on life.

St. Louis offered a number of empty buildings with architectural beauty. HRI estimated that at least fifty substantial, historic buildings, representing over ten million square feet of property, could be redeveloped. The state and city had already invested heavily in downtown. They had created the renowned Gateway Arch, the NFL Rams stadium, and a state of the art convention center. The city had also forged a broad plan to redevelop downtown St. Louis called "Downtown Now!" Central to it was creating a convention center hotel.

The new plan envisioned a twenty-four-hour neighborhood with residential and commercial development. As incentives for developers, Missouri passed legislation that authorized a 25 percent state historic tax credit. The cornerstone of the city plan lay in creating a one thousand-room, world-class, convention center headquarters hotel to replace a six hundred-room Sheraton Hotel that had previously served that role. The plan would locate the new hotel across the street from the convention center with its front door facing Washington Avenue, a corridor lined with historic building gems. The city put out an RFP, and HRI responded.

MEETING THE CHALLENGE

HRI's competition was Hellmuth, Obata, & Kassabaum (HOK) and its partner, Hilton Hotels Corporation. HOK is an international architectural firm headquartered in St. Louis that, ironically, had designed the New Orleans Hilton hotel for Lester Kabacoff. Its vision for the St. Louis project was to demolish historic buildings on Washington Avenue and replace them with a new hotel tower attached to the convention center. HRI's approach was to integrate the new convention center hotel into the historic fabric of the neighborhood, combining new construction with the preservation of the historic but then-vacant and blighted Statler-Hilton Hotel. Fortunately, HRI was selected as the developer.

HRI believed that winning the competition could accomplish four long-term goals: First, it could help revitalize downtown St. Louis. Second, it would establish HRI's first satellite development office outside of New Orleans. Third, it could demonstrate that the company was growing into a national player in hotel development. Finally, the hotel would enjoy huge financial success. The cost of the project exceeded $300 million dollars—nearly ten times the size of any previous HRI project. The complex financing used federal historic tax credits and Empowerment Zone bonds. The state provided funding for an 880-space garage, state historic and brownfield tax credits and contribution credits. The city provided over $80 million of loans and grants. Kimberly Clark Corporation provided tax credit incentive equity and traditional equity and became the project's majority owner. As the project's hotel brand, HRI chose the Renaissance, which Marriott had recently acquired for its upscale hotels. Marriott provided $10 million in loan funds and acted as manager of the hotel.

The project spurred a $5 billion redevelopment of downtown St. Louis, including an additional HRI project. HRI converted the former Merchandise Mart, another large historic building on Washington Avenue, into apartments. The combined impact of these two projects on Washington Avenue helped revitalize the historic center of St. Louis. Most of the empty buildings downtown have since been restored. A sustainable, vibrant, diverse neighborhood has emerged, and HRI helped make that possible.

These projects taught HRI much about complex public/private partnerships and neighborhood revitalization. The lessons learned were put to good use as it engaged in new ventures. Tom Leonhard's financial acumen was crucial. One of the great masters of slicing and dicing complex public financing, Steve Stogel, mentored him through the process. Stogel did not suffer fools gladly. His blunt approach made him difficult to live with, but on a complicated financing like this, he was impossible to live without.

The excellence of HRI's work on the Marriott Renaissance was manifest in the awards it earned. These include Landmarks Association of St. Louis Inc.'s 2003 Eleven Most Enhanced Sites Award; The Better Downtown Award for 2003 presented by the Downtown St. Louis Partnership; the Construction News & Reviews and National Association of Women in Construction Award for the historic rehabilitation of the Renaissance Grand Hotel; and the Renaissance Grand and Suites Hotels Phoenix Award 2004.

LIVE IT UP LIVE DOWN TOWN
436-6800

Aerial view of the Hilton Garden Inn Hotel and Gravier Place residential development.

HILTON GARDEN INN (FRENCH QUARTER / CBD)

New Orleans, La. **2004, 2013**

An unsightly parking garage topped by an empty 1960s office building blighted Gravier Street. HRI realized that revitalizing this building's façade and housing a hotel above the garage could change things and help create a dynamic neighborhood. The development demonstrated that even a non-classical, aluminum-clad building could be reconfigured as an attractive commercial development.

HISTORY

HRI built upon its success in the Warehouse District by focusing upon the Central Business District (CBD). Businesses that had moved to Poydras Street had left grand historic CBD buildings vacant. Pres Kabacoff and Edward B. Boettner learned that a one million square foot complex of buildings consisting of the First National Bank of Commerce, Richards buildings, and the Commerce garage were being auctioned off in Dallas. The auction was drawing bidders from all over the world. To ensure that only serious parties participated, a party had to submit a check for $50,000 merely to place a bid.

They attended the auction, held in a Sheraton Hotel ballroom. Fifteen minutes before the first bid, two brothers from India, Mohan and Gowri Kailas, approached them. "Do you want to bid with us or against us?" they asked.

Kabacoff and Boettner made a snap decision. A 50/50 deal was cut, literally, on the back of a napkin. They united, and the team's bid won. HRI led the conversion of the Richards Building into the Gravier Place apartments. Years later, it converted the Commerce Building into the Hilton Garden Inn French Quarter/CBD. Mohan Kailas converted FNBC into apartments known as the Four Winds, while retaining the FNBC bank on the ornately decorated first floor.

A HISTORIC ADAPTIVE REUSE

The Hilton Garden Inn is an adaptive reuse of the historic Commerce Building. Built in 1956 as an office building, it's located in New Orleans's Central Business District on the edge of the French Quarter. Abandoned and in bad shape, the project required a complete renovation. HRI persuaded the National Park Service that the building qualified as historic and was entitled to tax credits as an integral appendage to the FNBC and Richards buildings complex. The design team gutted the building above the garage and removed floor slabs to create a middle open atrium for seven floors. All elevators were rehabilitated. Floor stops were changed. A new entrance and lobby were designed for entry into the hotel lobby on the eleventh floor. The new hotel offered a business center, restaurant, meeting rooms, fitness area, and a rooftop swimming pool.

The hotel is located two short blocks from the French Quarter, with its fabled antique shops, grand temples of fine dining like Galatoire's, Felix's, and Arnaud's, art galleries, as well as historic homes and buildings. Serving a business and family clientele, the hotel has helped to revitalize a core area of the Central Business District that was abandoned by law firms, banks, commodities brokers, and other businesses who moved into newer Poydras Street skyscrapers or the Warehouse District.

The project sparked renovation of other office buildings into residential apartments and hotels. HRI President Tom Leonhard states: "There is a saying that New Orleans is the city that care forgot. Actually it's a city that cares a lot. So do its people. Some observers were prepared to write off this area as a lost cause. We took a positive view. Projects like this show that when care is lavished on abandoned buildings, providing new focus and creating activity within walkable distances, renovating old buildings into twenty-four hour uses such as hotel and residences can create a renaissance."

GRAVIER
PLACE
APARTMENTS
NOW
LEASING
504 679 5083

EXIT

A redeveloped unit of the former St. Thomas Housing Project, now part of the River Garden residential development.

River Garden

New Orleans, La. 2004-2009

New Orleans Irish Channel, circa 1920.

HISTORY

In 1937, his sails "full of the optimism of the New Deal," President Franklin D. Roosevelt signed the loan that enabled the St. Thomas Housing Development to be built. It was the first project funded under Senator Robert Wagner's Housing Act, whose mission was to provide public housing for low-income families. New Orleans desperately needed housing. The Depression had swelled the city's population. A 1937 "Report of the New Orleans Housing Authority" described living conditions in the city as rife with "desolation, despair, squalor, poverty, and frustration."[70]

The development originally covered ten city blocks and included 120 buildings. *The Nation* reported that the first family to move into St. Thomas included Mrs. Cecilia Booker and her children, John, Bettye, Sammy, Grace Lou, Henry, and Cecilia Oisonach. They moved in their furniture and built a fire in the fireplace and admired a new electric refrigerator in the kitchen. This stood in stark contrast to conditions in other low-rent housing neighborhoods that bore nicknames like Bedbug Row, the Buzzards, the Yellow Dog, Red Evil, and the Lizards.[71]

Segregation laws kept St. Thomas for white tenants only until the 1960s. The Civil Rights Act of 1964 ended that practice. St. Thomas's residential population became racially diverse as a low-income working class community. Eventually, several factors contributed to St. Thomas becoming a concentrated poor, impoverished African American community: white-flight to the suburbs; a federal requirement that residents of public housing pay 30 percent of their income in rent; and a decision by the U.S. Supreme Court, *Shelly v. Ferguson*, prohibiting discrimination against minorities in their housing choices.

The latter two had fateful consequences. Middle-income St. Thomas residents decamped to other neighborhoods, leaving the project a de facto segregated community. Single mothers, child abuse, and bad schools came to characterize St. Thomas. People subsisted in an atmosphere of fear and violence. Sister Helen Prejean described what St. Thomas became in *Dead Man*

The St. Thomas Housing Project prior to redevelopment.

The newly opened St. Thomas Housing Project, circa 1941.

Walking: "Not death row exactly, but close. Death is rampant here—from guns, disease, addiction."[72] Confronted by serious security challenges and a 75 percent vacancy rate, in 1996 the Housing Authority of New Orleans received a HUD Hope VI grant to rebuild St. Thomas.

The redevelopment of St. Thomas stirred huge controversy. The city wanted to break up the projects, which concentrated poverty in specific pockets. Plus, the footprint of the project dominated the physical, economic, and social landscape of the Lower Garden District. Life inside St. Thomas was inhospitable. In the two years before HRI was selected as developer, nineteen murders occurred inside St. Thomas.

The prevailing school of thought argued for ensuring that whatever came next have income diversity. A competing view worried that mixing low-income, jobless residents with strong middle class families would adversely affect stability and security. Noted sociologists like William Julius Wilson rebutted the latter view. He argued that mixed-income neighborhoods are healthier neighborhoods. In his view, "the basic institutions in that area (churches, schools, stores, recreational facilities, etc.) would remain viable if much of the base of their support comes from the more economically stable and secure families." It wasn't just middle or higher income people who worried. Low-income residents filed suit, complaining that the city's plan failed to address their needs. The suit, however, was dismissed, paving the way for redevelopment.[73]

THE BIRTH OF RIVER GARDEN

In the early 1990s, Pres Kabacoff had taken a close look at riverfront neighborhoods that wound the three miles from Poydras Street to Audubon Park. He concluded that stretch of land was healthy except for the St. Thomas housing project. The project housed five thousand lower income African Americans in 1,500 housing units spread among seventy different buildings. It was physically separated from the surrounding neighborhoods—essentially isolated. For all practical purposes, you could not drive into it. Most residents were women with children living on welfare.

Kabacoff invited former mayor Moon Landrieu, Reynard Rochon, and other community leaders to his home in the Fibre Mills building to discuss a way ahead. He believed that life in St. Thomas was bad both for its residents and the surrounding neighborhoods. They discussed breaking up the project and relocating its residents into some of the 37,000 abandoned and blighted houses scattered throughout the city, fixing those up, and providing a decent place for them to live. Coincidentally, community leader Tony Gelderman had a similar idea. "I thought," he says, "that we should do that, and renovate those blighted homes using funds generated from the sale of the property on which St. Thomas was located."[74]

Word of the meeting quickly got out. Skeptical African American community leaders summoned Pres to Kingsley House, a center for social services. They seated him in the center of the large meeting room, surrounded on all sides by forty people who were unhappy with what he had been doing. Community activist Barbara Majors opened up on Kabacoff. "Who are you to discuss the revitalization of St. Thomas without including its residents?" she demanded.

Kabacoff agreed. "You are absolutely right," he nodded.

At their request, he and his partner Ed attended Undoing Racism seminars. Afterwards, he thoroughly researched issues of poverty and housing. He paid special attention to the eminent sociologists and scholars William Julius Wilson, David Rusk, and Myron Orfield. Their work persuaded him that concentrated poverty in public housing produced family breakdowns, drug abuse, crime, bad schools, and other social ills. Their thinking proved prophetic. Soon after, the federal government created the Hope VI program that provided funding to de-concentrate poverty in public housing projects. The goal was to convert them into mixed-income housing with private rather than public housing management.

Aerial view of the sprawling St. Thomas Housing Project, circa late-1950s.

Units within the St. Thomas Housing Project immediately prior to redevelopment.

Onto this scene stepped developer and later President of the Urban Land Institute (ULI) Joe Canizaro, who owned land that bordered St. Thomas. He convened a ULI study team to make recommendations.[75] Vince Lane, an African American who chaired the Chicago Housing Authority and had earned national acclaim for sweeping criminals out of public housing, helped to lead the process.

Mayor Mark Morial liked the recommendations that emerged and applied to HUD for a Hope VI grant to revitalize St. Thomas. The Housing Authority of New Orleans (HANO) selected a large New York-based housing developer, the Starret Company, to get the job done. But things did not work out. Frustrated by local politics and inadequate public financing, a year and a half later, Starret backed out. A Florida-based housing firm led by Vince Lane replaced Starret. Unfortunately, Lane clashed with HUD as he tried to employ St. Thomas residents. That contract was terminated, also.

HANO rebid the project and selected HRI. The first challenge was financing. Morial had originally committed $17 million from the city for infrastructure improvements like roads, streets, and utilities. Constrained by tight budgets, he later advised Kabacoff that the city lacked the money to meet that obligation. Kabacoff found a solution after hearing a presentation by Harvard economist Michael Porter. Porter enjoyed an international reputation for his work on the theory of competition, and he had created an organization that focused on inner city competitiveness.[76]

Porter analyzed how a city could use its natural assets to compete for businesses and population that had exited to the suburbs. A key insight he offered was that "big box" retailers had overbuilt in suburbs and were looking to urban neighborhoods for new locations. In his view, big boxes could rebuild a city's tax base and provide inner city residents with ready access to retail stores and jobs.

Kabacoff was intrigued. He had to tread carefully. Getting St. Thomas revitalized required forging broad coalitions of support. But this was an era of rising neighborhood tensions, like when a bitter fight broke out between famous author and preservationist Anne Rice and Popeye's chicken magnate Al Copeland over Copeland's desire to decorate the front of his St. Charles Avenue restaurant with neon stars. It might seem trifling, but emotions ran high.

A more serious battle erupted in nearby Central City between African American pastors and preservationists. The issue was whether the grocery chain Albertson's could locate a 40,000 square foot "big box" grocery store in that neighborhood. The pastors and their flocks argued that their depressed neighborhood needed investment. Opponents argued that a big box store was inappropriate for historic neighborhoods. One preservationist went so far as to purchase a home in a key location that would prevent construction of the store. The house burned to the ground. Tempers erupted. Anger was wide spread. Racial tensions escalated.

Keenly interested in city planning and a conciliator, Councilman Oliver Thomas—an African American—called Kabacoff to find a solution. Kabacoff sought one by engaging with leaders of the New Urbanist movement.[77] He was especially interested in learning how to land a big box grocery in a historic neighborhood. The New Urbanists offered wise counsel. They cautioned against changing the fabric of the original street grid to accommodate parking. They advised organizing services like a hair salon, pharmacy, hardware, and non-grocery departments in a manner that created activity on the street and to which there was street access. Groceries, they advised, should be located in the store interior.

At Right: redeveloped units of the former St. Thomas Housing Project, now part of the River Garden residential development.

3

Public transit, a vital component to the revitalized neighborhood.

Armed with this information, Kabacoff enlisted the support of Preservation Resource Center Executive Director Patty Gay and its president, Henry Lambert, as well as African American pastors. An agreement was reached that cleared the way for Albertson's. Unfortunately, the company went bust and the store was never built. Still, Kabacoff's experience in helping negotiate a solution to Albertson's dispute helped him understand what it took to develop a big box store in an inner city neighborhood.

Mayor Morial liked the big box idea. He agreed that if HRI could make that happen, the city would dedicate the sales taxes the store generated to pay for the infrastructure improvements at St. Thomas. Armed with that, Kabacoff enthusiastically went out to recruit a store.[78]

He ran straight into a brick wall. National retailers shook their heads. As they saw it, New Orleans was too political, too poor, and developers aroused too much neighborhood opposition. Kabacoff sought advice from Darryl Berger, who had developed Wal-Marts in the western part of the country. Berger understood the importance of the St. Thomas redevelopment and volunteered to help attract a Wal-Mart. The two friends flew off in Berger's chartered jet to Bentonville, Arkansas, where Wal-Mart is headquartered.

It turned out that Wal-Mart executives had been trying without success to get its new "superstore" concept into an inner city. The concept combined groceries and dry goods. Taking a page from his Albertson's experience, Kabacoff insisted that any Wal-Mart store design had to satisfy two elements or face endless barrages of neighborhood fury. First, it had to respect the existing street grid. Second, it had to use a brick exterior that replicated the mammoth cotton press buildings that historically had dotted the Tchoupitoulas Street corridor along the riverfront.

Wal-Mart thought that made sense and agreed. HRI could now finance the project. Feeling the pressure lifted from his shoulders, Kabacoff expected his plan to generate approval. Instead, it ignited a new Battle of New Orleans. Preservation leader Bill Borah was among those who opposed it. Bringing in Wal-Mart waved a red flag to a preservationist bull. "This was a retail piece that was portrayed as part of a pedestrian scale, inner-city development. The pedestrian piece was a giant Wal-Mart with acres of surface parking. At the same time, Wal-Mart was beginning to use neighborhood markets. Why not use the smaller stores? The larger one was out of scale to the neighborhood."[79]

Kabacoff respected the preservationist perspective. But this time, he felt their vehement objections were misguided. Events have vindicated his judgment. Preservationists predicted that Wal-Mart would cause retail shops on Magazine Street to fail. The opposite occurred. Today, Magazine Street flourishes and is often compared to London's famous Portobello Road.

Walmart, the commercial anchor of the River Garden development.

"Here is the reality of Wal-Mart," Kabacoff says. "Historically, major retail was located in the city proper. Retail tax revenues generated half of its general fund. Flight to the suburbs and the ease of locating department stores and big box shopping there changed the picture. In the suburbs, zoning presented no obstacles. Parking was no issue. Losing retail and the taxes it generated to the suburbs like Jefferson and St. Tammany parishes had decimated city revenues. Transportation problems made it hard for low-income residents to have access to suburban shops and groceries."

In Kabacoff's opinion, "the only way to reverse the trend was to attract major retailers back to the inner city. This was delicate, as you want to avoid disrupting historic neighborhoods. Only an insensitive developer would try to put a Big Box on St. Charles Avenue. St. Thomas presented an opportunity thanks to its location next to the river amid mostly abandoned industrial land. There was plenty of space for the store and parking without disrupting the street grid or historic buildings. We saw the situation as a win-win for everybody."

Not everyone concurred. Lawyer and preservation leader Camille Strachan captured the feelings of many when she decorated her Lower Garden District house with a large banner that proclaimed "No Sprawl-Mart." Architect and former Coliseum Square Association President John Wettermark denounced the inclusion of Wal-Mart as "totally against all the things promised initially." The Association sued to block the project on grounds that no proper environmental impact study had been conducted, but courts dismissed the suit.[80]

Preservationists formed an unlikely alliance with affordable housing advocates to stop Wal-Mart. For different reasons, each sought to kill the plan. "The irony ran deep," Kabacoff says. "Although they had no problem with Wal-Mart, public housing advocates opposed any plan that provided for a preponderance of market rate units. They wanted mostly affordable-rate apartments. By contrast, many preservationists wanted mostly market-rate apartments. Feelings grew so intense that it was said the stage version of the controversy would be called 'A Streetcar Named No Thanks.'"[81]

Kabacoff shook his head, consoling himself with a remark that Senator John McCain had once uttered: "If you're getting flack from all sides, you must be over the target." He believed he was doing the right thing. "That's what gave me the confidence to persevere," Kabacoff added.[82]

Besides winning Morial's approval for the Tax Increment Financing (TIF), HRI needed the support of the City Council. The battle took on the characteristics of a political campaign. The city's major newspaper, the *Times-Picayune*, declined to endorse HRI's plan. Opponents were effective. They made it appear that a broad division existed in the community over the project. HUD Assistant Secretary Michael Liu threatened to pull the federal Hope VI Grant. He stated that the TIF to pay for St. Thomas infrastructure was, in his words, "smoke and mirrors."[83]

Kabacoff says: "Here was another lesson learned. When a bureaucrat unreasonably jumps in the way, go over his head and talk to the boss." Former Mayor Sidney Barthelemy, who headed up government affairs for HRI, set up a meeting with then HUD Secretary Alphonso Jackson. Jackson listened, overruled Liu, and green lighted the project.

In the meantime, City Council approval for the TIF was still required. To show depth of public support, HRI hired the respected pollster Silas Lee to conduct a survey of public attitudes and opinions. The poll revealed that only 10 percent of the public supported the opponents' position, but 69 percent agreed that revitalizing St. Thomas for middle and low-income residents, as well as for senior citizens and retail use, should be a top priority for city planners. Sixty-four percent said planners should make "attracting more retail stores such as Wal-Mart to New Orleans a top priority." The city council voted approval. That allowed HRI to complete the first phase of River Garden housing and construction of Wal-Mart. Future phases benefitted from federal financing that came to the state after Hurricane Katrina.[84]

No sooner was the Wal-Mart design done than the next challenge arose. HRI was an expert in historic renovation but had little experience in creating a newly constructed residential project. HRI sought more counsel from leaders of the New Urbanist movement. Kabacoff asked his team to read a book written by Andres Duany, who had designed Seaside, a well-known Florida community development.[85] Duany was a leading New Urbanist thinker. Kabacoff advocated the creation of walkable neighborhoods that combined shopping and entertainment as developed before the automobile, when people connected by using a streetcar. "One of the striking things is that the principles that guide New Urbanism define what New Orleans has been historically," Kabacoff said.

Kabacoff also brought in New Orleans architect Lloyd Vogt to teach HRI's architectural team how to design a New Urbanist community. Vogt had helped design the Rosemary Beach community near Pensacola, which employed New Urbanist principles.

The Times-Picayune
DAILY & BREAKING NEWS AT nola.com
Sunday June 9, 2002
75¢ · METRO EDITION

PRES KABACOFF WANTS TO PUT A WAL-MART IN A NEW ORLEANS NEIGHBORHOOD. AND THAT PUTS HIM AT ODDS WITH HIS OLDEST ALLIES: PRESERVATIONISTS.

THINKING OUTSIDE THE BIG BOX

By Elizabeth Mullener
Staff writer

When Anne Rice and Al Copeland got into a squabble a few years ago over the design of his St. Charles Avenue restaurant and hotel, everyone in town got a good laugh out of it, including developer Pres Kabacoff.

The novelist thought some standards of taste should have been invoked to preserve the splendor of the city's grandest avenue. The fried-chicken tycoon thought his aesthetics were just fine, thank you very much, and the neon stars he wanted to put on the front of his building were downright pretty.

"You could see these two characters on a comic book page," Kabacoff says. "Copeland versus Rice. It tickled me. You couldn't have dreamed it up."

Then came the Albertson's fracas.

"That was funny; this was bad," Kabacoff says.

The bitterness arose when the supermarket chain wanted to put a big-box store in Central City, and the preservationists went up in arms, calling for design modifications that showed respect for the historic nature of the neighborhood. Kabacoff got into that one, helping to arbitrate a deal he thought all the players could live with. It was a cautionary experience for him.

See KABACOFF, A-7

Storm clouds have rolled in for Pres Kabacoff. Long before he came up with the controversial proposal of putting a Wal-Mart store on the site of the former St. Thomas housing complex, the local developer, shown at the site of the planned store, was a man on the side of preservationists. With the new project though, Kabacoff has run into stiff opposition.

"All the News That's Fit to Print"
The New York Times
Late Edition
New York, Monday, April 21, 2003

Today, sun and some clouds, a spotty afternoon shower, high 72. Tonight, clear to partly cloudy, low 55. Tomorrow, partly sunny, high 76. Weather map on Page C8.

For Wal-Mart, New Orleans Is Hardly the Big Easy

By CONSTANCE L. HAYS

NEW ORLEANS

WHEN a local developer announced triumphantly that a new Wal-Mart would rise here on a sandy patch of earth along the Mississippi, it was presented as a good thing, a bit of progress that would bring in much-needed tax dollars and jobs and transformation where the rundown St. Thomas public-housing project once stood.

But along the way, someone overestimated the willingness of other New Orleanians to accept the advance of Wal-Mart across their turf. And one result has been a foul gumbo of accusations against everyone from the developer, once considered an urban hero, to the federal government, which made the grant that set off the fireworks in the first place. Themes of jealousy and betrayal have sounded over financing that gives the developer and **Wal-Mart Stores** — which wants to put up a 200,000-square-foot store plus a parking lot — unusual benefits. Lawsuits have been filed to block construction on behalf of the environment, the fabric of the city and the rights of the former residents of St. Thomas.

Jonathan Cohen for The New York Times

Maurice Pres Kabacoff, a developer, at the proposed site of a Wal-Mart in New Orleans. Lawsuits over the financing and other issues have delayed the project.

Wal-Mart is a cloud over Sysco, the leading food service distribution business. Page 4.

The back-and-forth, which began two summers ago, has been so intense and, in many ways, so particular to this place — the stage version could be called "A Streetcar Named No Thanks" — that the store is now more than a year behind schedule.

The struggle here is taking place as many of the country's big retailers, companies like **Costco Wholesale** and **Home Depot** as well as Wal-Mart, are reaching beyond their usual locations for growth. After saturating rural areas and edging into the suburbs, they are experimenting with ways to fit large stores into vacant inner-city acreage. It's not an illogical strategy, but as Wal-Mart is finding, the going can be rough.

"Nobody on the side against Wal-Mart is against jobs or against housing or against retail," said Neil Alexander, a photographer who has been a vocal opponent of the store. "What a lot of us are against is poor planning or no planning, and selling the city short to the largest corporation in the

Continued on Page 11

CREATING A DIVERSE, VIBRANT, SUSTAINABLE COMMUNITY

It's easy to get lost in politics while putting together community and political support to realize an idealistic vision. Looking back on the project, HRI President Tom Leonhard observes, "our company has a strong sense of community. Still, we're a real estate company. We finance and design. We build. We manage. Getting River Garden done required keeping that focus." Leonhard and Tom Crumley led the development team. David Abbenante headed up property management. Project Architect Gary Meadows oversaw the River Garden project from the initial HOPE VI grant application to the final phased completion ten years later. A first step, he says, "involved extensive master planning, wholesale demolition and new infrastructure design. The goal was to integrate a neglected, isolated neighborhood into the surrounding historic Lower Garden District and create a vibrant mixed-income community."

HRI built new homes in the architectural style of old New Orleans. They included Creole cottages, double camelbacks, and Greek Revival two-stories with columned fronts and double galleries. All the buildings are elevated two to three feet off the ground to avoid flooding. Each rests on a four-inch thick concrete slab foundation supported by concrete chain walls and twenty-five- to thirty-foot pilings. Apartments feature cutting edge solar technology. SolarEdge installed a centralized system that allows harvested energy to be monitored in real time. It sends web-based alerts on receiving faulty feedback, enabling engineers to respond quickly.[86]

HRI saved five buildings from the original development and reopened them with thirty-seven affordable housing units. It installed new plumbing and wiring, created new floor plans, repointed bricks, and re-created the floral ironwork to conform to their historic origins. HRI consciously kept the renovated buildings true to their original design. The apartments have high-efficiency air-conditioning units. Exterior staircases replaced the old rickety fire escapes. Three of these buildings surround a central courtyard shaded by four original oak trees. On either side stands a smaller building. These replicate the traditional layout for public housing built during the 1930s. The apartments vary in size between 540 and 915 square feet. They include two-level, two and three bedroom apartments as well as one and two bedroom units on the ground floor.

Today, River Garden has seven hundred apartments of which 60 percent are market rate and 40 percent are subsidized affordable housing. Residents facing St. Mary Street overlook a 2.75-acre park, today officially designated as Boettner Park to commemorate the work of Edward B. Boettner.[87]

Meadows notes that while public open space was a planning requirement, the designers ensured that the "final shape and character of the nearly three-acre Boettner Park maintained the mature live oak trees on the site. The traditional rectilinear street geometry was modified in this area around a concentration of trees to create a triangular park." In short, every step was taken to make River Garden attractive and livable.

RIVER GARDEN'S SUCCESS

River Garden has proven popular with residents. Commercial rental rates on Magazine Street, where merchants feared Wal-Mart would depress their prospects, have skyrocketed. Real estate expert Rick Stone observes: "When you've got a cluster of retailers in an area, it becomes even more of a draw for people where they can dine and shop and get a lot done. It benefits everyone there."[88]

Even a superficial look at the bustling, colorful array of small restaurants and shops that have sprung up along Magazine Street on the downtown side of Jackson Avenue all the way to Felicity Street vindicates that assessment. Indeed, says University of New Orleans professor and real-estate industry expert Wade Ragas, property values are up all over the neighborhood since River Garden has materialized.

River Garden residents brim with enthusiasm. Journalist Christopher Tidmore quotes one resident of the old St. Thomas project who walked into her new shotgun house in tears, declaring: "This is wonderful, more than I could have ever hoped for." She marveled at her new state-of-the-art kitchen, living room with paneled trim, new washer and dryer, and a small backyard—a luxury no resident of the old St. Thomas enjoyed.[89]

The project has drawn wide acclaim. Walter Gallas, director of the New Orleans office of the National Trust for Historic Preservation, told the *Times-Picayune*: "It puts the lie to the argument that 1930s public housing can't be rehabilitated. . . . I think it's amazing."[90]

FANNIE MCKNIGHT

Former St. Thomas Resident and Neighborhood Activist

Fannie McKnight is a representative of the St. Thomas Residents Council who once lived in St. Thomas. She was present and an active participant in turning the development into what is now called River Garden. Working closely with the late Barbara Jackson on the St. Thomas Resident Council, she served as an advocate for the people who lived in St. Thomas and still advocates for those who reside in River Garden. "People need an advocate," she says. "I take pride in playing that role. I help residents understand their rights as a resident, whether it's rents, utilities, or an eviction issue. The residents know they have a champion." But her dynamic activity helps HRI, because she is able to communicate clearly and forcefully the concerns of the tenants.

She's a mediator. She makes certain that all parties receive a fair hearing. She's bent on making certain that the right thing is done. She considers her forty-eight years of serving as an advocate her legacy. "I have a good relationship with Pres Kabacoff and HRI's managers, even when we get into hot and heavy sessions. I call the shots the way I see it. I let the residents know that they have rights, and if they are right, I stand up for them. If they are wrong, I say so."

When people need more space, she works with HRI to find them larger apartments. "You have to take into account the big picture and every little situation that fits within it. I make sure there is fair play. If a resident loses a job, I make sure they bring proof, and HRI will work with that person so they can keep their place to live."

HRI's management philosophy factors in accommodating residents who run into unforeseen problems. "The key," Fannie says, "is to keep talking, keep management in the know, get the facts. For example, if people complain that there are drugs on the property, I make certain that HRI calls that to the attention of the police. I let them do their job. If a person gets on drugs, I work to help them get help, with drug rehabilitation, so they don't get evicted and keep their house. That's what makes this work. Part of my role is to get the facts and make certain that HRI knows what's going on."

She's pleased that HRI has set aside Permanent Supportive Housing at River Garden and all of its mixed-income properties. PSH housing provides support for the homeless and hospice support for people who have terminal heart conditions or cancer yet have no place to go. Fannie worked to ensure that HUD designated St. Thomas as a Hope VI project. This ensured that former residents of St. Thomas enjoyed a preference in returning to what became River Garden. She has special praise for Hope House. "Hope House has been a big help in working with the homeless and residents in the community in helping with education and rents."

She is pleased at the way River Garden has lowered crime in the neighborhood. "We don't have so many killings in our community like we used to have. We can walk without fear for our safety. We still have crime in the surrounding area, but not in our development. Residents play their part. They come out when we hold events. HRI works closely with leaders in the community. It recognizes that the former St. Thomas residents take the lead. They fought to obtain the Hope VI funding that made River Garden possible."

Boettner Park, heart of the River Garden development, named in honor of HRI Properties co-founder Edward B. Boettner.

753
751
STOP

ANNE DAIGLE

Resident, River Garden

"I've been a New Urbanist for many years," says Ann Daigle, today a resident of River Garden. "I had followed the Hope VI project ever since they started with Henry Cisnero, the head of Housing and Urban Development. Hope VI took the place of the high-rise, concentrated projects in cities. The Congress for New Urbanism had been working with HUD to reform affordable housing. It worked to get HUD away from concentrate projects occupied by poverty stricken residents and into mixed-income and mixed-use developments."

She watched the redevelopment of the St. Thomas project go through all of its growing pains. "People fought back about tear-downs of historic buildings. Some didn't like the fact that Wal-Mart was part of it. The concept was brand-new even though it was based on old urban forms. The idea was to invigorate cities by replicating the way New Orleans really is, with mansions standing next to shotgun houses, drugstores near bars, small groceries and parks you can walk to. It's small scale mixed use. New Orleans has historically been famous for what we call that 'checker-board' housing pattern where rich live cheek-by-jowl with the poor. We're a gumbo. And New Orleans is a fabulous model for a development that captures that spirit."

Like all of the housing projects, she says, St. Thomas "contained multiple generations of people who lived in them. It was all they knew. Living in concentrated poverty is not good. That's why the mixed-income component is important. Having lived in New Orleans, it's amazing to see the interaction between myself and the children in what has become River Garden. It's healthy. It's good for everybody, I think."

She is a champion of River Garden. "First, the urban design is well done. I'm a professional urban planner. You have to respect HRI's conception and execution of the place. Out of all the developments in New Orleans, it most closely resembles the true character of the city in design and architecture. What I love is that they have mixed together different urban housing types. I live in a double-townhouse. We share a two-story building. That's what you see all over Uptown New Orleans—the classic two-story double. There are double shotguns, which is a single story house that has units on either side. There are side-by-side houses, such as you might find in the French Quarter, separated by party walls. And there is mixed tenancy. It's not just mixed-income, but mixed-tenancy, meaning you can buy or you can lease. River Garden offers opportunities to buy or lease."

Her praise for HRI is effusive. "The most important thing it does right is management: maintenance of the buildings and grounds, security, lighting. And there is strong racial diversity and that grows every year. The result is to provide stability and a strong neighborhood spirit. There are a lot of sponsored events in the park with music, food, [and] activities for the children. They do a quarterly newsletter that discusses issues of concern. It is true community bound by a strong neighborhood association."

The impact on the surrounding neighborhoods has been positive, in her view. "Everything around it has improved. We do have our problems. Some adjacent property owners refuse to maintain their properties. I'm hoping that HRI and other parties find a way to reach out and include the surrounding residents and businesses in the success achieved in River Garden. They've done a great job and I have high hopes for the future."

Daigle looks at similar projects around the country. "This is the only one that has already built out its retail components. This is growing stronger every year. What's great is you can walk to stores. You don't need to own a car. Within a quarter-mile walking radius you can take care of all your daily needs."

CAMILLE STRACHAN

Attorney and Neighborhood Preservationist

Camille Strachan built her professional reputation as an attorney in private practice, litigating zoning issues and providing advice on corporate and civil matters. With her gregarious warmth and a life of passionate commitment to renewing New Orleans, she is an icon in the city's preservation community.

"What first drew me to neighborhood preservation was the old houses. Then when I married Duncan Strachan, whose parents had been early preservationists, I began to understand the importance of the whole fabric of an area. In the late 1960s, Magazine Street between Washington and Jackson avenues was in the doldrums," Strachan states. "During that time, they restored four properties which stabilized that strip and led to the restoration of other properties. Their efforts engendered a sense of hope for the future."

She and Duncan found a beautiful Greek Revival brick house between Euterpe and Polymnia streets on Coliseum Square in the Lower Garden District. The house emerged as a headquarters for neighborhood activists who saw the beauty of the surrounding neighborhoods after the State Department of Transportation proposed to place a new access to a second Mississippi River Bridge in the middle of the neighborhood. "It was a sign of how absurdly insensitive government could be in taking actions that could wreck a historic neighborhood." The neighbors worked with a coalition of people that included Councilman Eddie Sapir, State Representative Dorothy Mae Taylor, and other residents to block the initiative. When Louisiana's colorful—and very powerful—Governor Edwin Edwards forced the Department to listen to reason, the initiative died.

During the 1990s, it became increasingly clear that the nearby St. Thomas Housing Project was causing huge problems for both its own residents and the adjoining neighborhoods. "I was of the opinion that the St. Thomas buildings merited renovation for mixed-income housing. The argument we heard from HRI was that renovating them was too expensive and that the better idea was to demolish and replace them. And that's what happened, except for thirty-seven units that were preserved," she recounts.

Inevitably, plans to redevelop St. Thomas set off emotionally charged arguments. Overwhelming public support for replacing St. Thomas drowned out the voices of those who opposed its demolition and relocation of residents. Where the sparks flew was over what to replace it with. At one point, Camille acted briefly as the lawyer for the St. Thomas Residents' Council. In that capacity, she advocated for clarity about what might happen to the residents.

"One of the biggest problems is that residents felt they had no control over their lives or what would happen to them. As their counsel, I sought transparency and openness from the city and prospective developers as to their plans," she states.

The politics was complicated and nuanced. Politically powerful pastors outside St. Thomas felt their voices should be heard on dealing with residents. Social activists asserted their views. In the view of some, the voices of the residents themselves got lost. Those who subscribed to this conclusion argue that outsiders who had never lived in the project positioned themselves as the authorities to speak for residents. In their view, the political leadership found it easier to deal with them than the residents' council. "It was my view the city's political leadership put its head down and kept on going. It tended to ignore the feelings of St. Thomas residents," Strachan says. "But the train was leaving the station and the one thing that no one could accept was the status quo."

After HRI was awarded the contract to redevelop St. Thomas, more controversy embroiled the development when HRI proposed the construction of a Wal-Mart. Camille provided a visible presence in the debate. She strongly opposed the Wal-Mart. "I felt there was a chance it might harm Magazine Street and that the tax increment financing on the site was a sweetheart deal for Wal-Mart. It seemed that instead of getting a concern that paid taxes like other businesses, the city was giving away the store." Today, looking back in retrospect, she acknowledges that Magazine Street is flourishing. "And because of the opposition, the city wound up with a better looking Wal-Mart. I'm pleased that the store reflects the historic sensibility of nineteenth-century cotton warehouses in that area."

Since Katrina, she points out, "the urge to live on the higher ground near the Mississippi River has revitalized all of the surrounding neighborhoods, including the Lower Garden District and the Irish Channel. The revitalization of St. Thomas almost certainly helped facilitate that."

Main entrance of the Bywater Artist Lofts.

Bywater Artist Lofts

New Orleans, La. **2008-11**

HISTORY

The Ancient Order of the Krewe of Kolossos is a wonder. The centerpiece of HRI Bywater Art Lofts, the whimsical floats attached to tricycles standing beneath a spray of color streamers and the Krewe's Mardi Gras emblem are led by a fierce black bull with white horns, a white nose, startling blue eyes, and a cheerful expression. Companions that follow him include a superb pelican with an enormous beak and yellow eyes highlighted in black, white, and orange, a green grasshopper, a seductive pink and yellow unicorn, an endearing dragon, and an American eagle with wings decorated in the colors of the U.S. flag.

Beside this magnificent spectacle stand the lofts populated by artists offering "bearded oysters," a blue-and-white shark's head, a cut-out of Superman and Casper the ghost, and an awesome Rube Goldberg puzzle. There are trees, benches, and a five-foot cigarette sitting atop a silver filter tip.

Molly Gardner, the talented bass player, vocalist, and artist whose medium is circus banners made from recycled drop cloths, manages the lofts. Her face lights up every time she talks about them. "We have culinary artists, dancers, card readers, visual artists, writers—artists living together in a community atmosphere in the Bywater neighborhood," she says. "People are very, very focused on what they are doing. The ages cut across the board, from twenty to sixty. But what's so exciting is the kinetic quality that gathering so much high-powered talent sparks."

Bywater rose like a Phoenix in the wake of ruins left by Hurricane Katrina. Historically a blue-collar community, Bywater's affordable housing had traditionally offered a haven for artists, and many French Quarter workers lived there. While the storm damaged or destroyed 200,000 homes, Bywater sits on high ground and was protected from major flooding. Most of its housing remained intact, but rent prices skyrocketed, making it unaffordable for low-income residents. There were a number of large, vacant manufacturing facilities, however, and HRI recognized that converting these buildings into artist housing would give the area a strong boost.

HRI's Vice President of Development Josh Collen says: "Abandonment doesn't intimidate artists. They're true pioneers. Their energy and creativity sparks life wherever they live. We knew a project geared to artists could stand up Bywater and help restore its vibrancy."

Minneapolis Artspace had proven the viability of using affordable housing tax credits for artists. HRI had also employed the concept in Shreveport and Hammond, Louisiana. HRI President Tom Leonhard recognized that artist housing well-suited Bywater, and HRI identified two historic industrial buildings there to renovate for artist housing. These became the Bywater Art Lofts and Bywater Art Lofts II. The properties had once served as the site for the legendary Rex Garment factory and warehouse on Dauphine Street in New Orleans. The J.H. Rex Rutter Manufacturing Company had built the factory in the 1920s to produce Army uniforms. The same factory inspired John Kennedy Toole's fictional Levy pants factory portrayed in his Pulitzer-prize winning novel *A Confederacy of Dunces*.

Floats from the Ancient Order of the Krewe of Kolossos.

THE BYWATER NEIGHBORHOOD

Bywater exemplifies the changes brought on by the post-Katrina arrival of a creative class seeking historic properties on high ground near the Mississippi River. The Industrial Canal, Press Street, St. Claude Avenue, and the Mississippi River frame Bywater's boundaries. Adjoining the high-priced French Quarter and the chic Marigny neighborhoods, Tulane Professor Richard Campanella identifies two factors that have driven Bywater's gentrification: historic properties and proximity to other gentrified areas like the French Quarter.[91]

Gentrification was coming to Bywater in the 1980s, as people converted double houses into single-family dwellings and increasing rents pushed out lower income residents. Campanella reports that the speed at which this shift in demography has occurred is surprising. Their "magnitude and velocity may be extreme in the metro area," he says. By 2010, the population had declined by a third, from 8,939 to 5,915. The shift saw a dramatic change in the racial composition, as the African American population dropped by about half, while the white population grew by over 20 percent.[92]

In Campanella's view, the shift had less to do with race and more to do with income and education. "The process of gentrification is the movement of a wealthier demographic into any area that was working class or poor to some degree," *Times-Picayune* reporter Doug McCash quotes Campanella as stating. But, the Tulane scholar points out, "change has defined New Orleans through most of its history."[93]

The revitalized Bywater neighborhood along St. Claude Avenue.

One challenge that rising rents posed was that higher prices deprived artists of a place to live. HRI felt that artists are important to building a neighborhood, and Bywater had historically served as a home for their community. It saw a need to provide affordable housing in the neighborhood from which Katrina and rising rental prices had displaced them.

THE DEVELOPMENT OF THE LOFTS

Artist Molly Gardner had been living a block away on Dauphine Street when Josh Collen approached her about managing the project. For Gardner and Collen, it was a leap of faith. She had no management experience. Indeed, she observed, "I'd never held a regular job before. I had no formal qualifications, no training. Josh's offer was amazing. Needless to say, I did what artists always do. I jumped in with both feet."

The neighborhood was seeing tough times. Shops and stores were closed. The warehouses were considered dangerous. "We called it Rainbow Alley because rainbows had been painted on the walls of buildings," she said. "It was just ominous. An entire block with two blighted buildings face to face. It was kind of frightening." The buildings then consisted of rusted metal, broken windows, buses parked in the front yard, and vine-covered heavy-timbers. Collen characterized the place as "dilapidated, blighted, [and] an absolute mess." But he maintained his vision of turning the spaces into housing for artists.

Ernest Ward served as architect of record for the first phase, Bywater Lofts I. Michael Albracht of HCI Design—HRI's in-house design studio—did schematic designs. Bywater Art Lofts revitalized the garment factory. Bywater Art Lofts II renovated the warehouse located across the street.

Collen credits Michael Albracht with the creative vision. Says Albracht: "Our philosophy rejects building for the sake of development. We wanted to be a good neighbor. Our goal was to help the neighborhood." Designs provided a lot of parking and bike racks. "It turned out," he grins, "that parking was no problem. What residents wanted were bike racks. Of course we obliged."

The Bywater Neighborhood Association worried about how affordable housing might impact the neighborhood. HRI assured neighbors that residents would be artists and good neighbors. "We also agreed to give preference to artists for the apartment units," Josh Collen says. "It was a promise that came with an unexpected obstacle. After construction had started, the Internal Revenue Service insisted that we could not use Affordable Housing Tax

Atrium of the Bywater Artist Lofts.

Credits that way. Since the credits were vital to financing, we needed a solution. HRI and Artspace took the case directly to Congress. They argued that nondiscriminatory artist housing would foster neighborhood revitalization. Congress agreed and amended the law. Today, the Low Income Housing Tax Credit program permits giving artists a preference for such units."

Kabacoff also demonstrated his commitment to the neighborhood by building his own quixotic home next door to the Bywater Art Lofts. "Bywater is a truly great historic neighborhood," he notes, "and we love living there." The first lofts proved such a triumph that the Bywater Neighborhood Association strongly supported the second.

DESIGN

For the Bywater Art Lofts, the building interior was gutted and new floor plans established. The building incorporated an industrial element, with exposed ceilings and ductwork, sealed concrete floors, and brick walls. A community area located in the center of the building gave artists a place to work and display their art. Exterior restoration reused and replaced windows to match the existing steel windows on the building. Brick and metal façades were restored and a new apartment storefront was installed. New sidewalks and parking lots accommodate tenants.

Bywater Art Lofts II occupies a 1950s warehouse structure across the street. Behind a neutral beige exterior lies an open interior parking lot that the *Times-Picayune* calls "a feast of geometry, with blood-red iron trusses rainbowing from one side to another and glinting galvanized staircases declining from each second-story apartment to the ground." Apartments have high ceilings and spacious windows that create a sense of space and light. Lofts II offers on-site parking, bicycle storage, gallery space, and a common studio space.[94]

Albracht and the design team tailored units to how artists live. The open floor plans let residents informally personalize their space. "We integrated as much natural light as possible," he explains. "Some units lack exterior windows. We addressed that by placing windows that looked onto a spacious, well-lit interior atrium or using solar-tube skylights." Artists have special requirements for floors. They did not want to worry about problems like paint spilling on a carpet. "We decided that newly poured and sealed concrete was right for aesthetics and durability," Albracht says. "Concrete floors are flexible. The second floor had original timber. We covered those with easy-to-clean vinyl." Plumbing was placed in the center of each unit to increase efficiency.

THE ART GARDEN

Occupying a double lot across from Loft II, the garden is intended for the primary use of Lofts residents. Albracht notes: "We have a platform that can be used for performances. We have trellised areas, landscaped areas, [and] a garden for growing produce." HRI chose local artists to create the art and sculpture that anchor the garden: Paul Fowler contributed a mammoth twenty-foot tall Phoenix from reclaimed metals that came from demolition work on Bywater Lofts II; James Bella offered up a fanciful glass flower bouquet; Shae Freeman designed a steel sculpture she calls "horse whips," a dramatic, towering bouquet, with nine structures that shoot straight up from the flowerpot like bamboo; and Aria di Capo fashioned a concrete flower sculpture. The two metal gates reflect the Lofts' industrial heritage. Local metalsmith Rachael David forged them out of wrought iron. "She's just incredible," Gardner says. "We told her it was a Rex Garment Factory. She ran with the idea. You can see buttons, even seam work in the material."

Bywater Art Lofts created thirty-seven units and Bywater Art Lofts II an additional thirty. "Working artists of all disciplines are eligible," Collen says, "as long as their income is within the $27,000-$37,000 range. We welcome any artist who meets that criteria and has a portfolio. We render no judgment about the art itself. That's for collectors to decide." Applicants receive apartments on a first-come, first serve basis, after HRI verifies that they meet income requirements.

REVITALIZATION ACHIEVED

The two buildings that comprise the Lofts project stand as an important reminder of the time when the city had a vibrant manufacturing industry. Eddie Boettner takes a special pride in the two Lofts buildings: "New Orleans is an artistic community. It's very satisfying to provide affordable lofts that enable artists to thrive and prosper."

Atrium of the Bywater Artist Lofts.

BYWATER
ART
LOFTS
3725 DAUPHINE

At Left and Above: the Bywater Art Garden.

KING EDWARD HOTEL AND STANDARD LIFE LOFTS

Jackson, Miss. 2010

"Downtown Jackson, Mississippi, is like an old fashioned iron weight-lifting barbell," Pres Kabacoff muses. "The bar itself is Capital Street, which runs through downtown. The city's high-rise buildings line this corridor. At one end stands the historical Greek Revival state capitol and government complex. The other end was a graveyard for dilapidated historic high-rise properties, including the King Edward Hotel and the Standard Life Building."

Designed by William T. Nolan, the King Edward Hotel in Jackson once reigned over the city's life. R.O. Edwards built it in 1861 on the site of the Confederate House. In 1863, it burned down. The Edwards House followed in 1868 and, in 1923, the current building.

Nolan used a neo-classical revival style with the front façade featuring a limestone portico of coupled Corinthian columns. These support a full entablature and balustrade that shelter the Capitol Street entrance. The lobby was distinguished by six large columns set along the perimeter of an oval light well, lit by skylights above the second floor.

For decades, the hotel was a social, economic, and political hub of Mississippi, serving as a coveted venue for weddings, dinners, and other celebrations. State legislators attending sessions in the state capitol proudly called it home. A reporter once wrote: "There are three branches of the Mississippi Legislature—the Upper House, the Lower House, and the Edwards House."

In 1955, the owners renovated the hotel in a modernist style and renamed it the hotel King Edward. They replaced its grand marble staircase with an escalator and covered over historic details such as the lobby rotunda.

Closed in 1967, the hotel was abandoned to vagrants, vandals, and pigeons. In 1976, the vacant building was placed on the National Register of Historic Places. In 1990, the Mississippi Department of Archives and History designated it a Mississippi Landmark. By 1999, the building was ranked among the state's 10 Most Endangered Historic Places.

Beginning in 2006, HRI and developer David Watkins teamed up with former New Orleans Saints running back and Jackson native Deuce McAllister. Two previous developers had failed to find sufficient financing. What the project required was a state incentive for historic renovation. HRI, Watkins, and McAllister went to the legislature and persuaded it to create a state historic tax credit that covered the project. Using that, federal historic tax credits, and new markets tax credits, they were able to acquire and revitalize the King Edward into a hotel and the Standard Life Building into apartments.[95]

They combined the properties into a single project, with HRI serving as the Managing Member of the King Edward Revitalization Company. Among the team leaders for HRI was Hal Fairbanks, who today serves as Vice President for Acquisition. Looking back on the project, he makes a key point about HRI: "HRI has often been the developer of last resort. We specialize in saving iconic buildings from the wrecking ball and developing them into major new projects that draw strong community support. Our ability to gain access to lower cost capital sources provides HRI an edge in identifying new opportunities that contribute to a city's sustainable future. King Edward epitomized our success in achieving that goal."

At Left: the Standard Life Lofts with the King Edward Hotel in the distance.

KING EDWARD

The King Edward was converted into a Hilton Garden Inn. The hotel's deteriorated condition made it difficult to use many of the building's original materials, but HRI salvaged what it could. The historic spaces of the hotel were restored to their original grandeur, including the lobby, rotunda, pre-function spaces, and the neo-classical exterior.[96] Modern amenities such as a basement pool and fitness center and residential amenity deck were designed to integrate smoothly with the hotel's historic features.[97]

The completed project has 186 hotel rooms and 64 luxury apartments, seven thousand square feet of conference space, a restaurant, and a bar. The hotel also has a coffee shop. A 158-space parking garage services both the hotel and the apartments. HRI's Josh Collen aptly sums things up: "King Edward ranks among the most important buildings in all of Mississippi. Our renovation of it has proven a catalyst for reinvestment in the entire area."

Exterior (at left) and lobby (above) of the King Edward Hotel.

Rooftop pool of the King Edward Hotel with nighttime view of Downtown Jackson, Mississippi.

STANDARD LIFE

Renovation of the Standard Life Building began while the King Edward was still under construction. Designed by noted Jackson architect Claude Lindsey, a cylindrical tower tops the narrow building that first bore the name Jackson Tower. Upon completion, it became the largest reinforced concrete building in Jackson—and the tallest. Vertical massing and surface ornamentation of angular geometric forms characterize its exterior. The art deco lobby features marble and terrazzo finishes with geometric patterns.[98]

It opened in 1929 after being constructed in five and a half months using twenty-four hour shifts, six days per week. Built as a speculation, it attracted all sorts of tenants, including insurance companies, dentists, and oil companies, yet until the 1950s, the federal government was by far the largest tenant. The building was home to the Bureau of Public Roads, the Veterans Bureau, the Department of the Treasury, and the WPA. Standard Life Insurance Corporation acquired the building in 1951. Later, InterContinental Life acquired the company but moved its operations to Philadelphia, leaving the building nearly vacant. Upon its acquisition, HRI renamed it the Standard Life Apartments. Today it contains seventy-six residential rental apartments on eighteen floors and 2,671 square feet of retail space. HRI modernized the building with new plumbing, mechanical, electrical, life safety, and roofing systems.

HRI worked closely with the National Park Service and the Mississippi Department of Archives and History to respect historical accuracy. It engaged the Heritage Consulting Group to ensure that renovations complied with federal and state historic guidelines. "The King Edward was a legendary hotel in Jackson," said Heritage's Cindy Hamilton. The renovation has restored that luster. She also noted that the Standard Life Building is a significant "example of art deco skyscraper construction." HRI viewed renovation of the Standard Life building as complementary to the adaptive reuse of the hotel and as a stimulus for downtown Jackson. The upscale units are fitted out with major kitchen appliances, high-speed internet access, a state-of-the-art fitness center, on-site property management, security, and access to hotel services and amenities. Large windows and ten-foot ceilings afford stunning views of the city.[99]

The *Jackson Free Press* honored the renovation as the best change to the city in 2010. Hilton Hotels singled it out as the best hotel conversion of the year. The National Trust for Historic Preservation awarded it its Preservation Honor Award. The elegant $120 million project epitomizes the HRI philosophy of creating diverse, vibrant, sustainable communities.

Nighttime view of the Standard Life Building.

Front and side view of the Blue Plate Artist Lofts.

Blue Plate Artist Lofts

New Orleans, La. 2011

"We had a vision," said developer Tara Carter Hernandez, as her JCH Development, LLC, teamed up with HRI Properties to renovate the vacant Blue Plate factory into artist lofts. Their goals: revitalize New Orleans's Gert Town neighborhood that stood directly behind the building and restore an iconic New Orleans building to create affordable live/work spaces for artists. They viewed artists, who are often urban pioneers, as a key to rejuvenating a less affluent neighborhood that Katrina had severely damaged. "Artists make a neighborhood hip and cool, gentrified," Hernandez says.[100] The original Blue Plate building, designed by architect August Perez in 1941 in the Art Moderne style featuring curving forms, horizontal lines, and rounded glass-block corners, fit the bill perfectly. Pres Kabacoff loved the project. From his early childhood, he had regarded Blue Plate's unusual art deco neon mayonnaise sign as one of the city's three most memorable visual landmarks, in company with the Hibernia cupola, which is illuminated in colors that reflect special holidays, and the Falstaff Brewing Company tower, which used the vertical letters of the brand name to provide weather forecasts.

AN ADAPTIVE REUSE

The Blue Plate Artist Lofts is an adaptive reuse of a building that stood vacant until 2010. HRI's Development Project Manager Kirsten Vaselaar reports that after Katrina, "the building was so empty we could see from one end of the first floor to the other." Respected for maintaining high standards while working quickly, Woodward Design + Build was selected as the contractor. Woodward Senior Vice President Bill Hoffman notes: "We worked closely with JCH and HRI to integrate design and construction on a tight schedule."

Construction requirements were exacting. A survey revealed that the 1941 industrial steel windows could not be rehabilitated. Woodward coordinated with Graham window manufacturer to create replicas that were energy efficient and could withstand hurricane-force winds. Bedroom walls in the apartments varied, so Woodward trimmed the millwork to fit the different shapes of individual walls precisely. The concrete floors transmitted a lot of sound, threatening privacy. Woodward innovatively solved the problem by placing a sound mat beneath three inches of polished concrete that was poured on top. In addition, solar tubes created a high-performance day-lighting system.

The building's interior highlights its industrial past. The factory floor layout was preserved, with broad open spaces punctuated by a grid of structural concrete columns. The layout of individual apartments was designed and built to highlight these columns in living spaces. Polished concrete floors and exposed concrete columns and ceilings create an industrial look. Historic glazed tile was salvaged and re-installed in key locations for residents to better understand the building's historic function. Innovative walnut blasting removed lead paint without damaging the underlying concrete ceilings.

"The project incorporated green building elements, making it a historic renovation with an emphasis on sustainability," Kabacoff explained. Woodward CEO Paul Flower is equally proud of the green features. "We installed energy efficient windows, Energy Star appliances, high efficiency HVAC systems and low-flow plumbing fixtures. We used sustainable construction materials. Rooftop solar panels increased sustainability and lowered utility bills," he states.

Excellence is apparent inside and outside the lofts. Artist Madeleine Faust created the building's backlit, glass-block sculpture that graces the front lawn. She also created the central fountain in the rear courtyard that is constructed from the building's original pipes and fittings. The design team created a perimeter fence for the site using bricks from two small warehouses that were demolished on the back of the site. These creative uses for original materials provided a sense of place and incorporated the building's historic past.

They maximized the space inside to form a central atrium that houses another Faust sculpture near the ceiling, made of fiber optics and LED lighting. A large ball with planetary spikes absorbs daylight and glows at night. The ball used to hang in the freezer of the Blue Plate test kitchen and the spikes were mayonnaise-tasting pipettes.[101]

Resident Roger Hahn praises the twelve-foot concrete exposed ceilings that "imparts a sense of grandeur" to the apartments. Says Hahn: "The designers were even careful to paint the tiny, front grill of the industrially exposed air duct hanging from my ceiling—all confirming a sense that the entire space is its own work of art."[102]

CAPITALIZING ON SOLAR ENERGY

Soon after Katrina, Pres Kabacoff attended a meeting of civic leaders who were interested in revitalizing New Orleans. Their key concerns included the fact that New Orleans faced a long-term threat from rising sea levels and the subsidence of land. By 2050, the city could well be situated on the very edge of the Gulf of Mexico. Levees are designed to protect against storms, not the Gulf lapping up against the city's edges. The group recognized that New Orleans would rank among the first major U.S. cities to confront this threat, posed by global warming and soil subsidence. Not far behind are New York City, Miami, Norfolk, and many other coastal cities.[103]

This concern led Pres Kabacoff to conduct in-depth research into renewable energy and green building practices. In testimony before the New Orleans City Council, he argued for a more robust "net metering system" to compensate residents who install alternative energy systems such as solar panels. At the Council's urging, Kabacoff assembled an Energy Policy Task Force to make recommendations for a sustainable energy policy. These recommendations led the Council to adopt the city's Energy Smart Program.

HRI's River Garden development, which revitalized the former St. Thomas Housing Project, became the state's first apartment complex to use solar energy. River Garden was a demonstration project. Its success prompted HRI to embark upon a $10 million effort that installed solar energy on rooftops on selected HRI apartments across Louisiana. To make that financially feasible, Donald Sylvester identified energy grants that helped fill financing gaps.

Many HRI projects have flat roofs, including the Blueplate building. HRI's utilization of the Blueplate's (and other projects) flat roofs for large solar installations illustrates the company's commitment to the employment of innovative alternative renewable sources of energy.

AN AESTHETIC ACCOMPLISHMENT

Journalist Carol Pulitzer praises the Blue Plate Artist Lofts, writing that "aesthetics rule here, guided by the motto 'Live, Create, Inspire.' Poetry benches designed by Barbara LeBlanc dot the hallways along with vintage Blue Plate

Main entrance of the Blue Plate Artist Lofts.

Blue Plate Fine Foods building, circa 1940.

photos brushed onto aluminum. Bicycle racks are pipe-bent into the letters B and P, artists hang their work outside their apartment doors, and the S-shaped stairwell banisters read like a grand treble clef note." Rents are affordable. The grounds feature three oak trees and an expansive front lawn.[104]

How successful was the project? "The seventy-two-unit lofts achieved full occupancy and a 1,300 applicants waiting list within four months of completion," HRI Co-Chairman Eddie Boettner says with a broad smile.

Kabacoff and Leonhard are especially pleased the project spurred new investments for single-family housing in the neighborhood. "Tara and our entire team shared a vision to improve the city. We went the extra mile," Leonhold says, "meeting with residents in the neighborhood, addressing concerns and even holding a job fair to extend work opportunities." The developers felt a strong social responsibility to support local small, minority and women-owned businesses—and they delivered. "The job fair was a huge success," Kabacoff reports. "Indeed, 83 percent of new hires on this project were classified Section 3 employees from the local community. Disadvantaged, Minority and Women Business Enterprise and Veteran Owned Small Businesses did almost 27 percent of the work." [105]

The lofts are located at the central, triangular intersection of three major New Orleans streets—Earhart Boulevard, Washington Avenue, and Jefferson Davis Parkway. Hernandez got the area formally designated as a Louisiana Cultural District. That step helped artists by eliminating retail taxes on all art sales and spurred development in surrounding neighborhoods.[106]

Respect for historic architecture and sustainability in innovatively adapting an industrial plant for artist lofts earned the Blue Plate Artist Lofts an Association of General Contractors (AGC) award for excellence. The building is individually listed on the National Register of Historic Places, and all work satisfied the Secretary of the Interior's Standards for Rehabilitation of Historic Properties.

Tom Leonhard puts it this way: "We restored an abandoned Streamline Moderne industrial building and transformed it into a unique space in which the imaginations of artists are free to soar, while providing a catalyst for surrounding neighborhoods to thrive and prosper."

Rear gallery of the Blue Plate Artist Lofts.

Side view of the Blue Plate Artist Lofts, with iconic neon sign.

Rear courtyard of the Blue Plate Artist Lofts.

Rear view of the Blue Plate Artist Lofts.

BLUE PLATE
BLUE PLATE

EXIT
DANGER
CAUTION
FORK LIFT
AREA
EXIT
EXIT

HIBERNIA NATIONAL BANK

HIBERNIA BUILDING MIXED-USE DEVELOPMENT

New Orleans, La. **2012**

During the 1970s, New Orleans experienced an oil and gas boom. Major national developers like William Hines and important local entrepreneurs like Joseph C. Canizaro built towering skyscrapers along Poydras Avenue. These gleaming structures attracted a lot of businesses that had previously occupied stately buildings, such as the First National Bank of Commerce Building and the Hibernia Bank Building.

By the turn of the twenty-first century, much of the original Central Business District was emptying out, lifeless and nearly devoid of major business. The area was in danger of becoming a ramshackle neighborhood right in the middle of downtown New Orleans. New Orleans faced a divided business district. Poydras Street was modern and housed banks, law firms, shipping businesses, accountants—the heart of commercial enterprise. The area between Poydras and Canal Street featured Class C office buildings that were classically built and could be adaptively reused as residential, hotel, and office space, as well as ground-floor restaurants and retail stores. In short, the historic part of the Central Business District was ideally suited for revitalization into a walkable, dynamic neighborhood.

HISTORY

A Louisiana landmark for generations, the Beaux-Arts twenty-three-story Hibernia bank building was built in 1921. At 355 feet in height, it stood as the tallest building in Louisiana until 1932, when the state capitol in Baton Rouge was completed. It remained New Orleans's tallest building until 1967, when the World Trade Center captured that title. It was renowned for its high-tech secure vault with a forty-eight-ton door that a team of mules had transported from the riverfront. A copper time capsule remains among the artifacts exhibited in the bank lobby.

Designed by the architectural firm of Favrot & Livaudais, it is constructed of a steel skeleton with a light-gray Indiana limestone sheathing. Massive Corinthian columns line the building. The Greek Revival white cupola atop the building was once a navigational beacon for ships, and at one point the belvedere was open as a public observatory. During World War II, it served as a lookout point to watch for enemy ships that might come up the Mississippi River. On top of the cupola was a broadcast antenna used by New Orleans's first television station, WDSU. The cupola is lit at night. On most days it is in white, but for holidays it is lit in representational colors: At Christmas the lights are red and green; for St. Patrick's Day, they're green and white; at Mardi Gras they turn purple, green, and gold; and on the Fourth of July, they're red, white, and blue.

The ground floor bank lobby has impressive scale and elegance. It features polished floors and tall, fluted travertine Corinthian columns on all four sides of its grand lobby. A large brass chandelier hangs from the ornate ceiling.

Capital One acquired ownership when it purchased Hibernia Corporation in 2006 and continues to operate the ground floor as a bank. Hibernia and other firms that had offices in the building have decamped for new quarters.

Ornate main lobby of the Hibernia Bank Building.

NEW LIFE FOR A LANDMARK

In 2011, a joint venture comprised of HRI and Woodward Interests, Inc. purchased the building. They renamed it the Hibernia Tower Apartments. Their vision was to give the building and surrounding area new life. A $58 million renovation adapted the building into two levels of Class A office space above the ground floor bank space and 175 mixed-income apartments.

Realizing big dreams never comes easy. Putting the project together required over five years of hard work. "We faced a lot of cost challenges," HRI President Tom Leonhard said. "Builders faced a tough economic environment. Financing required a mix of equity from federal new market tax credits and federal and state historic state tax credits, a Capital One loan, and an Industrial Development Board PILOT incentive."[106] "Contractors had to work double time to make deadlines," Pres Kabacoff recalled. "Every day was a race to the finish. We worked very closely with Paul Flower and his Woodward team to make it happen. The results speak for themselves."

Gary Meadows led the architectural team, which defined the key goals for design: HRI would preserve the iconic look of the building; it would respect historic spaces in the building, like the cupola and bank floor; and it would assure high quality while revitalizing a building and placing it back into commerce. It was always recognized that Capital One would retain its ground floor bank branch.

Iconic New Orleans streetcar passing in front of the Hibernia Bank Building.

HRI chose to use the second and third floors for its own headquarters. For that space, the team created a barrel-vaulted clerestory in the open office area. The original wood paneling and bas-relief ceiling of the Hibernia Bank Board room were left intact while lighting, AV, and mechanical upgrades were incorporated. Interior workspaces salvaged brass gates and featured new glass art. Wood paneling in corner offices was left intact and gypsum board with recessed lighting replaced dropped ceilings.

The apartments above are luxuriously appointed: GE stainless steel kitchen appliances; granite kitchen and bath surfaces; oversized closet spaces; hardwood flooring; and expansive windows in living rooms and bedrooms. The original windows were able to be maintained but were retrofitted with weather-stripping and film to enhance thermal efficiency. Each unit features direct ducted, outside air preconditioned and heated using natural gas. Amenities include a fitness center and a rooftop pool, as well as an attached 114-space parking garage with additional spaces for bicycles.

A REVITALIZED DOWNTOWN

"The project," Tom Leonhard stated, "well expressed our vision to transform commercial downtown into a walkable neighborhood where people can live, work, play, and visit." The Hibernia aimed to draw a diverse range of occupants. They include market rate, moderate income, and workforce level tenants. Even before completion, all the units were rented and there was a four hundred-person waiting list. Leonhard was pleased to see his prediction that if you build great places to live, people will come: "Getting an iconic building up and running, and creating a new community of residents downtown does the city an awful lot of good. And it makes us feel good about what we do and why we do it."

Winning the Down Town Development NOLA award for Best Development Project of 2013, the project realizes HRI's vision of walkable livability. Located on the St. Charles Streetcar line, the Hibernia Apartments lie within easy walking distance to the French Quarter, Lafayette Square, the Superdome, Harrah's Casino, the Riverwalk, the Algiers Ferry, the bio-medical district, City Hall, and the bustling retail shops and restaurants that have transformed New Orleans's Central Business District day and night.

Architect Gary Meadows smiles broadly as he considers what the HRI-Woodward team achieved. "In its previous life," he says, "the building served as offices. People went home after work, leaving it vacant at night. We gave it new life. It has a lively residential community. Activity flourishes day and

The Hibernia Bank Building, circa 1930.

night. People here are defining a new lifestyle in which they live and work in the same area. New Orleans is a city of life and this project has helped to assure that reality."

Hibernia's renovation capped the change in the historic central business district. It signaled that the most visible, prominent building in the city had come alive. It assured that revitalization would be permanent. Eddie Boettner liked the Hibernia project so much that he has taken up full-time residence there. "I can walk everywhere," he says. "I love to walk to restaurants. I love to hear the rumble of the streetcar."

Boettner touts the impact the project has had on the historic CBD: "We've brought 175 new families to this neighborhood. They support groceries, restaurants, entertainment. They add nightlife. And because there are more people, their presence enhances safety." Thirty years ago, this part of the business district was dead after 5:30 p.m. Now it is alive, bustling with energy.

The iconic cupola of the Hibernia Bank Building illuminated with distinctive colors signifying the Mardi Gras season.

Strand Apartments / Aloft Hotel

New Orleans, La. 2014

The former 225 Baronne Street building—now the Strand Apartments and Aloft Hotel—stands on a street at the lakeside edge of the Central Business District. Most of the major buildings on the street, including the First National Bank of Commerce and New Orleans Public Service, were blighted. HRI had previously renovated the Richards Building into the Gravier Apartments on the river side of Baronne Street. By itself, this project failed to create the street activity required to be perceived as a walkable neighborhood. HRI concluded that bringing 225 Baronne back to life would provide a sufficient critical mass of vibrancy on the street. A series of developers had tried and failed to renovate and adaptively reuse 225 Baronne. The keys lay in solving the parking problem and bringing in historic tax incentives.

What others had overlooked but HRI realized was that the building had historical importance beyond it age and qualified for historic tax credits. Architect Gary Meadows solved the parking problem. At one point, his offices were located in what is now the First Bank and Trust Building on Poydras Street, looking out directly over the Baronne Building. Meadows recalls:

> I noticed that at the rear stood a nondescript two story structure located between it and the New Orleans Exchange Building. The next day I toured the small building. I realized that by acquiring the site, we could create a parking garage ramp structure, which would allow access to the first ten floors of the building for parking. That was the lynchpin that made the entire project feasible. It also created an opportunity to locate a hotel pool and pool deck on top of the parking garage. It also enabled use of the second floor roof of the parking ramp structure to house mechanical equipment. All of this meant a huge cost savings in construction and service expenses. The idea worked. The owner of the small building wanted parking space. We wanted a parking garage. There was something for both parties. We got lucky.

Obtaining tax incentives required looking beyond the architectural details. The building had a "brutalist" exterior and aesthetically would not at first glance qualify as historic. HRI placed its significance in a historical perspective. It was the first major building built in the historic CBD after World War II. It helped maintain and expand the downtown economy as flight to the suburbs dispersed business to the city's perimeter, where land was more available and easy to reach by automobile. The growth of suburban neighborhoods and shopping malls had accentuated that trend. The building stood as a counter to the flow of businesses to Poydras Street. It has also played a key role in transforming New Orleans's skyline from mid-rise buildings to high-rise structures. HRI got the property listed on the National Register of Historic Places. Historic listing brought an additional $30 million in historic tax credit financing to the project.

THE REVITALIZATION

Once the home to Boeing Corporation, Chrysler, Entergy, and the Jones Walker law firm, the building is a thirty-story steel-frame high rise clad in brick and glass. At a cost of nearly $100 million, HRI renovated the structure into a mixed-use development for a hotel, parking, and apartments.

The Starwood Aloft Hotel features 188 rooms. The apartments are mixed income, with 20 percent of the 192 units designated for affordable housing. The units boast hardwood floors, stone counter tops, and stainless steel appliances. There are two pools, one for hotel guests, and the other for apartment residents.

The tower's tripartite composition, constructed with steel and concrete, qualify it as an example of New Formalist design. At its first floor base, a chrome canopy floats horizontally above Minoan black columns and a recessed aluminum storefront. Its middle section alternates vertical ribbons of aluminum windows set in rough, brown brick with projecting headers between pilasters of glazed white brick. A floating roof caps the entire trapezoidal monolith. Aluminum screens with circular motifs cover vents at a second floor mechanical mezzanine. The existing features make it a very typical work of its architects, Shaw, Metz, and Associates of Chicago. New Orleans has other outstanding examples of this style in its Public Library (1958) and Auto Life Building (1963), each designed by New Orleans's architects Curtis & Davis.

THE SETTING

The setting of 225 Baronne is dense and urban. Buildings of comparable use—both newer and older—surround it. Two blocks downriver lies Canal Street, which has historically served as the downtown shopping area for the city; three blocks upriver lies Poydras Street, along which stand high-rise towers and the Superdome; and eight blocks away, the Mississippi River flows. In the aftermath of Hurricane Katrina, numerous Central Business District buildings situated on the lake side of St. Charles Avenue buildings sat completely or partly vacant. Some had become blighted even before Katrina.

HRI co-founder Pres Kabacoff saw the project as a cutting edge example of HRI's philosophy of smart growth for sustainable communities. "Ignored after Katrina, 225 Baronne injects new vitality into the historic Central Business District," he says. "The large number of units and a stylish hotel creates density and activity."

HRI Vice President of Development Josh Collen feels 225 Baronne development represents a major advance for the area: "It places New Orleans squarely in a national trend that sees people returning to urban centers closer to where they work." Apartment broker Larry Schedler offers insight into why the project is attracting so many new residents. These inner city residents could easily own homes in the suburbs but, he points out, "would rather rent in an area that is the center of activity."[107]

Prices are lower compared to similar properties in other cities. HRI Management President David Abbenante notes that the company capitalized on that. Plus, he states, "there is a deep thirst for high quality living spaces that place folks in a high energy area that lies within walking distance of the French Quarter and work places. The New Orleans Warehouse District, the Museum District, and the developing South Market District are becoming one distinct neighborhood."

LIGHTING UP THE TOWN

More than a place to live, HRI aimed to make the Strand a landmark that adds to the festive spirit of the CBD. While the rooftop is usually lit up each night in cobalt blue, an automated system has twelve programmable light or color sequences that affords the ability to display solid colors for events such as breast cancer awareness. HRI plans to vary the colors for other events. The lights enable the Strand to stand-out from other buildings and embellish the skyline.

REVITALIZING THE CENTRAL BUSINESS DISTRICT

The flow of residents into the historic CBD has been transformational. By 2015, a handful of major new developments were underway. These included the New Orleans Public Service (NOPSI) building, the Pythian Temple, the Oil & Gas Building, the Rault Center, and 111 Tulane Avenue. HRI Project Development Manager Richard Allen summarizes the achievement: "The 225 Baronne Building continues HRI's mission. It is leading the way in restoring livability and vibrancy to that area of the CBD that lies along the Baronne Street corridor. Even a lane for bicycles has been added."

"Like the Hibernia's renovation into apartments, the Strand epitomizes a resurgence," says Kurt Weigle president & CEO of the Downtown Development District. Both buildings provide the creation of new housing in the middle of the Central Business District. The impact is clear. There is the old adage: retail follows apartments and hotels. As the downtown population in the CBD grows, more demand is created for retail and service outlets. That is critically important for redeveloping Canal Street up to and beyond its previous glory.[108]

225 Barrone Street during construction, circa 1961.

Rooftop pool of the Strand Apartments with view of the French Quarter and Mississippi River.

ANGELA MITCHELL LEBOEUF

Penthouse Resident, The Strand

"I'm a true New Orleanian," said the red-haired Angela Mitchell LeBoeuf, in her black and gold jump suit. The colors reflect the uniquely Crescent City affection for its football team, the Saints. She graduated from West Jefferson High School, Phillips Community College, and Delgado Community College. She and her husband own and operate L&L Marine, a tugboat company.

They are also residents of the sparkling high-rise on Baronne Street that has taken the name the Strand. "We put up our house for sale. We hadn't sold the house yet. I started looking at apartments. We had a 4,000 square foot house in English Turn. It was too much. We wanted a more carefree lifestyle. If the lights blow out, we wanted to call someone and know they'd be here in an instant to fix it." She looked at a number of apartments. Then she saw the billboard that's off the Interstate by the O'Keefe exit that advertised the Strand. "It looked just like I wanted it to be," she said. "The blue lights beneath the roof top caught my eye. And I said: 'That's it. That's where I want to live. In the heart of the CBD.'"

They moved in during June 2015, on the first day it opened. "We wanted a penthouse. That we could get a penthouse apartment with a terrace was unheard of. I got the amenities, a view, and terrace. Who could ask for more? It was exactly what I wanted. My husband feels just as excited." She says this with a grin. "I have to say, he didn't start out that way. He was pretty skeptical. We were in a temporary apartment at first, until our penthouse was completed. He wanted his outdoor space. You feel the vibe. Everything changed the day we moved in, and he is so happy."

What does she like about the Strand? "The people," she declares. "The people who work there are amazing. They get everything done. They help you with packages, with mail problems, anything that needs to be taken care of, they assist you with a smile. They clearly love their job and they are there to help. They show you that they are there for you. From day one, I felt that way, especially with the manager, Brenda Wright. The leasing agent, Martha Eager Allen was fabulous. She handled everything for our moving from the temporary apartment to the penthouse. Everyone is accommodating. If you have a problem, they're right there to take care of it."

The building attracts a very diverse set of residents. "There's every age group, every race, every style of person. It's a totally eclectic mix and I love it. It's very New Orleans, actually, because that's the way New Orleans is. People from different backgrounds, living side-by-side, becoming friends, being good neighbors."

She loves the fact that that the Strand is centrally located. "There's so many restaurants. I'm a self-proclaimed foodie. And I'm loving walking everywhere, to all of my favorite restaurants." She singles out Revolution, G.W. Finn, and Willa Jean. "But there's so many restaurants popping up right where we live."

KRISTI TAGLAUER

General Manager, Aloft New Orleans Downtown

I was born in Hickory, North Carolina, one of six. Two boys, four girls. People called us the Taglauer tribe. But we lived all over. My dad was a teacher and when I was ten, he became a pastor. I've lived in seven different states. I graduated from the University of New Orleans with a degree in hotels, restaurants, and tourism.

We had moved to New Orleans while I was a senior in high school. I started college a semester early. I had wanted to be a doctor and started out in pre-med. Then I got a job at the Royal Sonesta Hotel to earn money for tuition. I found that I enjoyed serving people. The hotel business was exciting. You met celebrities. There were exciting activities. I was working in the heart of the French Quarter. For a Midwestern kid, that was pretty exciting stuff.

I worked my way through college and worked briefly at the Sonesta. That led to work at Holiday Inns. I met my mentor there: Maureen Lauden. Marureen was the general manager at the Holiday Inn & Holidome in Kenner, Louisiana. She was inspirational—a great teacher and coach. She allowed me to work in a lot of departments. I got to experience food and beverage, sales, [and] front office—the big picture of managing a hotel. I loved it.

From there, at the ripe old age of twenty-eight, I became a general manager at the Holiday Inn Covington. Today, I'm the general manager at the Aloft hotel at 225 Baronne, which HRI owns. I had worked with HRI for eight years previous to taking on this assignment. The Aloft is an energized environment. There are so many puzzle pieces that have to fit together that make a hotel run—housekeeping, engineering, food and beverage, accounting, you name it. There's something for everybody. I enjoy being the head coach. I love organizing the departments and making them work well together. In the most positive way, I'd describe what we do as a puppet show. We make a lot of moving pieces fit together for the entertainment, convenience, and pleasure of our guests.

I love my work. But I confess, I strive to achieve a healthy balance between work and home. Managing a hotel keeps you inside. When I'm playing, I like to do things outdoors. I love gardening. I love beach volleyball. I love bicycling. The Ozarks are a paradise for people like myself, who like to camp. But when you step back, what gives me the most satisfaction in life is helping people. Aloft provides a perfect venue for doing that.

wxyz

aloft
wxyz

Marais Apartments

New Orleans, La. 2014

During the 1970s boom times (before the oil companies decamped New Orleans for Houston) Texaco ventured to upper Canal Street to construct a twenty-one-story skyscraper. When the bust came, leaving New Orleans in serious decline, Texaco joined the exodus to Texas. Upper Canal Street became a fulcrum of surface parking lots and blighted buildings. The Texaco building would remain dilapidated and shuttered for seventeen years. No one wanted to work, shop, live, or go there, unless to park.[109]

When HRI won the contract to revitalize the Iberville Housing Development and the surrounding neighborhood, questions arose as to where Iberville's elderly residents could be conveniently relocated. HRI concluded that the solution lay in revitalizing the Texaco into apartments for them, but the development sparked controversy.

Some objected that affordable housing on Canal Street would continue the street's demise. HRI knew that family housing in a high-rise was not practical. Experience has shown that family housing in high-rise buildings is difficult to manage and to maintain as a safe place to live. But HRI's experience with developing elderly housing at Redemptorist, Flint-Goodridge, and Mater Dolorosa showed that Texaco was ideal for the elderly. It was near retail shops, hospitals, and public transportation, and it could be managed as an attractive living environment.

HISTORY

The Marais Apartments occupy the former Texaco Oil Company building designed in 1951 by Charles E. Hooton and recognized as one of the earliest International Style skyscrapers in Louisiana. The style epitomized 1950s skyscrapers. The structure has a welded steel frame that was innovative for that era. The use of lighter steel, as opposed to concrete, allowed office spaces to be open and flexible, unconfined by cumbersome interior support columns. Hooton incorporated other innovative features, including its HVAC and chilled water systems, recessed lighting, and a curtain wall with glass façades. The exterior façade displayed green enamel panels—a take off from Texaco's logo of the time. Use of that material for an office building was rare.

The Texaco Building, circa early-1960s.

Tulane's school of Environmental Health and Tropical Medicine occupied the seventeen-story Texaco Building until Hurricane Katrina, when it evacuated, leaving the surrounding area lifeless until the state built the new Bio Science Center Building on an adjacent lot on Canal Street. The question then was, what to do with a tired, empty Modern International style building. Because the Texaco building was listed on the National Register of Historic Places as symbolic of commercial structures of over sixty years ago, approvals for any renovation had to be obtained from the National Park Service, the New Orleans Historic Landmark Commission, and the Louisiana Division of Historic Preservation.

HRI developed a fresh design concept that would adapt the building to provide residential housing for elderly residents while maintaining the historic 1950s character and aesthetics. Architectural Project Manager David Maise's vision was to create in modern architecture an echo of post-World War II America, simulating a 1950s and 60s era that featured young Americans working in a modern building.

Especially exciting to the design team was the opportunity to provide housing for seniors who had once resided in the nearby Iberville Housing Development. The Marais Apartments provided breathtaking views of the city they live in and love. These views overlook the river, French Quarter, Tremé, and the Central Business District. Maise's vision was for residents to see and appreciate "the unity, the city of vibrant and sustainable communities."

FOSTERING A REBIRTH

Various design challenges confronted the effort to transform a commercial building into residences. Property lines that bounded three sides of the building created issues of access and control. Asbestos and lead had to be removed and Katrina damage repaired. New structural supports also had to be added.

The design team included HRI Properties as the developer/owner, HCI Architecture, LLC as architect of record, Landis Construction Co. as the design build contractor, and Rick Fifield as the historic preservation consultant. The team sought to fashion a work of architectural art. Stacking window on top of window created a vertical ribbon. The vertical fins adjacent to the windows served as attachment points along with horizontal stabilizers to create an aluminum and glass curtain wall. The major challenge of Hooten's early design was keeping water and wind out of the building.

New HVAC systems were designed for each apartment and for ground floor commercial spaces. New plumbing, electrical, and fire protection systems were installed. Existing terrazzo flooring on the ground floor was restored along with the stainless steel elevator. From design to completion, the design team achieved the goals it had set for form and function that met historic requirements.

A self-contained structure, the building footprint is fully used and boasts an emergency generator sized to handle required life/safety equipment, emergency lighting, and elevators. The fourth floor boasts an activity room equipped with a computer room and garden terrace. In addition, there is a community room, beauty salon, and laundry room. Some second floor units have an open-air terrace with wood decking and three units on the second and third floor have a private interior light well. The property has one hundred one-bedroom and twelve studio apartments, all reserved for residents sixty-two or older.

REVITALIZING A NEIGHBORHOOD

The first phase of HRI's Iberville-Treme Choice Neighborhood Project, HRI viewed the Marais Apartments as more than a renovation. The building is positioned in the Downtown Development District and surrounded with points of interest. The Bioinnovation Center, Tulane Medical Center, the Saenger Theater, Canal Street, and the Vieux Carré are adjacent. Stores and restaurants are an easy walk away.

David Maise proudly recalls holding a vintage photograph of the building from the 1950s and standing in the same spot from which it was taken. It was a thrill, he says, "to see the building façade come to life, restored to its original state. It was a *modern* pierce of architecture, rebirthed, saved, restored, redeveloped, whole once again in form and function."

Canal Street near the Texaco Building, circa late-1950s.

JACQUELYN HUGHES MOONE

Resident, Marais

Jacquelyn was born in New Orleans, but she spent most of her life in California between Los Angles and San Diego, leaving New Orleans when she was about ten years old. In California, she became a professional dancer. "I did it all, but my favorite was modern and jazz. I became a choreographer and director of a high school dance company."

She visited New Orleans throughout her life, but after Katrina, "I felt an obligation to come home and see how I could help. There was a poignant need for people who were not here during the storm to return. You can only do so much from a distance." Like so many New Orleanians who leave for much of their lives, Jacquelyn came home. "I was part of a huge migration of residents who wanted to live again and to be an active part of the community," she says.

Seated during her interview in an eclectic colorful Bohemian ritual attire that is as vibrant as her personality, she talked about what it is like to live in the Marais Apartments. "It's an interesting mish-mash of personalities, education levels, and neighborhoods all joined together. It presents moments of challenges as well as a lot humor. But there is a common denominator aside from our being all seniors. People are passionate about what they are focused on. I think that reflects the diversity of neighborhoods from which they come."

Most of the residents have college educations and professional backgrounds. "Some were business owners, even those whom one might term 'working class.' They operated small businesses. They thrived in the hospitality industry. We have Vietnam vets. We have some who were once homeless."

"You're never bored unless you want to be," she laughs. "Many residents are defiant in how people view them as *seasoned*—I use that word, not *seniors*—because we are not grey-haired children. We're not geriatrics. We're very active. The eldest person in the building is ninety-four years old. The second eldest is ninety-two. They're probably our most independent and feisty residents. They both led very full lives. One was a dancer and a singer. These days she collects antiques. The other is a church-going lady whose always scolding her adult-age kids for standing over when, as she reminds them lovingly, she's perfectly capable of taking care of herself.

"Everything is there for us. People think that getting older makes you think old. That's ridiculous. Our age gives us a richer, fuller appreciation of life—a little more lagniappe, a little more cayenne."

Mooney considers the Marais beautiful. "It's like somebody loved their grandparents a lot and transferred that love to us. I have a beautiful view. Living two floors from the top, I call my apartment the 'near penthouse in the sky.' I can see the French Quarter all the way to the river. I see beautiful sunrises and the boats on the Mississippi. But living at this height, I don't have all the downtown noises that [can] be disruptive.

"On the ground floor, there's a gallery. I'm the curator. We call [it] 'Rhythm & Hues at 1501.' We show work from everyone from Jamar Pierre to Sondra Blakely, both of whom enjoy national reputations. Terrence Osborne is a New Orleans artist with an international standing. My own work also goes on display. We feature new, emerging, and established artists. It serves both our tenants and the greater commercial community."

101
MARAIS
APARTMENTS

Rooftop view from the Texaco Building overlooking a revitalized Canal Street.

Redeveloped units of the former Iberville Housing Project, now part of the Bienville Basin residential development.

BIENVILLE BASIN

New Orleans, La. 2015

The Iberville Housing Development sat cut off from the street grid. Despite its downtown location next to the French Quarter, Canal Street, and major hospitals, it isolated its residents from the city. Businessman Michael Valentino, whose family owns and operates four hotels in the Quarter and three downtown, observes that it "created safety issues internally and for the surrounding neighborhoods. It was 60 percent vacant and poorly managed. There were some number of visitors from other parts of the city every day and every night who had various agendas in the surrounding neighborhood. I thought the complex was in a state of decay and was socially volatile." Many residents shared his concern.[110]

Kurt Weigle, the president and CEO of the New Orleans Downtown Development District, feels that "the greatest economic impact of Iberville on the surrounding neighborhoods was probably more in how it was perceived. But never underestimate that. The fact was, having a nine hundred-unit public housing project situated on the edge of downtown next to the French Quarter held back downtown's development. The city recognized the need for redevelopment. The result is Bienville Basin. Its residents deserved better housing and redevelopment would create new opportunities for them and other citizens across the city."[111]

HISTORY

The Iberville housing development opened in 1941. It was situated on the site of the infamous Storyville red-light district that was once home to not only numerous brothels, but theaters, music halls, and saloons. Some residents had roots six or seven generations deep, as the area was home to free men of color even before the Civil War. Non-residents called it Iberville—the first letters rhyming with "crib." Residents insisted the first letter rhymes with "eye." Either way, they developed a close-knit community. "Children with no blood kin became cousins and neighbors considered each other family," said Ed Buckner.[112] Collaboration made housing developments cultural hotbeds. In the early twentieth century, jazz developed in the area and from its residents.[113] By the end of the century, Iberville and other housing projects continued to influence music. Travis "Trumpet Black" Hill said: "If it weren't for the projects you wouldn't have a James Andrews, a Trombone Shorty, or a Trumpet Black." Projects were the home-turf of up-and-coming rap, hip-hop, and bounce

Children at play in a courtyard of the Iberville Housing Project, circa late-1930s.

The sprawling Iberville Housing Project, circa late-1940s.

artists: D.J. Jubilee, Katey Red, and Mystikal in St. Thomas; Juvenile, Birdman, Lil Wayne, and other Cash Money artists in Magnolia; Master P and his crew in Calliope.[114]

The neighborhood was also famous for gumbo, voodoo, jazz, and civil rights pioneers. Louis Armstrong once walked in the streets and delivered coal as a boy. One of the last Storyville buildings standing, Frank Early's Saloon on Crozat and Bienville, was the go-to corner store, dispensing candy, snacks, and cigarettes at all hours.[115]

The original aim of public housing was to provide affordable places to live for those in need. The real growth came after World War II, as government acted to provide homes for returning soldiers. But by 1988, a report commissioned by Mayor Sidney Barthelemy determined that all of New Orleans's public housing was unmanageable and beyond repair. Social activists like Nora Goddard acknowledged that such complexes "bred unhappiness and crime through their layouts, their locations, and their management and lack of maintenance."[116]

French Quarter blogger Thom Kahler described the Iberville complex as "the criminals gateway to the French Quarter" and "that crime hellhole." Tyrone Yance, spyboy for the Yellow Pocahontas Indian Tribe, witnessed murders, kidnappings, and stabbings. "And I saw that by 10 years old," he recalled.[117]

Iberville was the last of the six large public housing developments in the city to be revitalized. Although dramatically less controversial than the demolition of St. Thomas and other housing projects, this redevelopment did spark some complaints. Goddard worried that taking down the housing project would unfairly displace its low-income residents. Association of Community Organizations for Reform Now organizer Wade Rathke branded the project "cultural tourism." In his view, it meant advancing business interests at the expense of low-income families. Treme community activist Jerome Smith complained, "we are allowing ourselves to be erased."[118]

New Orleans business leaders felt differently. They viewed Iberville's redevelopment as pivotal to revitalizing Canal Street.[119] Champions of redeveloping Iberville observe that the project will connect Iberville and Treme with the city's downtown business district on Canal Street and revive neighborhoods that had become hotbeds of crime, drugs, and poverty. "We're building it back better than it ever was before and the way it always should have been," Mayor Mitch Landrieu has stated.[120]

Aerial view of the Iberville Housing Project just prior to redeveolpment.

PLANNING THE FUTURE

Pres Kabacoff is an inveterate city planner. HRI had led the revitalization of Lower Canal Street—Rampart Street to the Mississippi River—by converting the abandoned 600,000 square foot D.H. Holmes complex into a hotel, apartments, retail, and parking; HRI's focus then shifted to Upper Canal—Rampart to Claiborne Avenue. The Iberville Housing Project, the closed Jung Hotel, and a plethora of ugly surface parking lots blighted the area. Even before Katrina, as a civic matter, Kabacoff had developed a vision for revitalizing the center of downtown New Orleans.

His vision encompassed the then under-utilized Charity Hospital (which was put out of service by Katrina), Iberville public housing, and Upper Canal Street. He ranked center city revitalization as equal in importance for the city's future to the construction of the Superdome, developing the Lakefront into new neighborhoods, and revitalizing the riverfront. Adds Kabacoff: "Every thirty or forty years we do something dramatic in the city."

To articulate the vision, he created a PowerPoint presentation that used aerial photography. He showed it to anyone who would watch, including then Lt. Governor Mitch Landrieu. Landrieu's response startled Kabacoff. "Pres," Landrieu declared, "you're thinking too small." Landrieu suggested that he broaden his center city vision to encompass everything from Interstate 10 to Louis Armstrong Park/Treme.

"Mitch was right," Kabacoff comments. "He understood cities and he's a big thinker. His advice caused us to expand our own vision." The PowerPoint renamed the plan for "an Afro-Caribbean Paris." Kabacoff's first objective was to revitalize the Iberville Public Housing Project. Both mayors Marc Morial and Ray Nagin had turned thumbs down to the idea, but Mitch Landrieu threw his support behind the idea upon reaching the office. Kabacoff also showed the plan to David Gilmore, whom the new HUD Secretary, Shaun Donovan, had assigned to administer the New Orleans Housing Authority.

Donovan brought a delegation of federal administrators to meet with Mayor Landrieu and key members of the city's leadership. HUD wanted to see how they could help New Orleans in the wake of Katrina. Donovan's number three, Fred Tombar, was from New Orleans. He asked Kabacoff to present his ideas for creating a place-based neighborhood in the Iberville and Tremé neighborhoods.

Shortly afterwards, HUD replaced the Hope VI program with a new HUD Choice Neighborhoods Initiative program. Hope VI addressed only the public housing project. Choice expanded the program to embrace the surrounding neighborhood and its people. Six cities received HUD Choice Neighborhoods Initiative grants. New Orleans was among them. The city and its housing authority selected HRI and McCormick Barron Salazar to present its proposal to HUD to obtain a Choice neighborhood grant. Kabacoff used the Afro-Carribean PowerPoint presentation. The city was selected. HRI and McCormick Barron Salazar were then designated to redevelop Iberville and the neighborhood around it and to provide services for the residents.[121]

THE GENTRIFICATION ISSUE

Iberville, which HRI renamed Bienville Basin, cast into high relief the debate over gentrification and how one achieves vibrant neighborhoods. Some argue that revitalizing historic neighborhoods presents a draconian choice that selects gentrification over affordable housing, which is untrue. Gentrification means improving a neighborhood to attract residents who are middle income and above. Such residents restore and improve buildings and the surrounding environment. Still, gentrification creates a challenge. When homes are improved, property acquires greater value and less affluent residents can no longer afford to live in the neighborhood. The solution does not lie in discouraging improvement. That's self-defeating. What's required is identifying a way to support the working poor so that they can afford to remain in their neighborhood. Several alternatives can achieve that goal.

One is subsidized affordable housing. In the Bywater neighborhood of New Orleans, which saw extraordinary gentrification after Katrina, HRI converted abandoned industrial buildings into seventy-four subsidized artist housing units. That was more affordable housing than anyone had ever done in that neighborhood. None of these units are market rate; they are all subsidized even though the quality of each unit equals that of a market rate unit. A second option is to require "fair share housing." That entails setting aside a percentage of housing units in any new development for low-income residents. Given the inadequacy of affordable housing, a third approach is for the federal government to double the amount of money it makes available to subsidize it or to enable a person to move to a new neighborhood of their choice (e.g., a voucher). There is no getting around the reality that such housing requires government subsidy.[122]

Emotions run high in this debate. That became especially true as New Orleans decided to redevelop blighted housing projects. The naysayers were misguided. Dismantling public housing as we knew it has created fresh hope. The public housing projects had concentrated the poor. Crime, violence, bad schools, child abuse, and other social ills riddled the places. Residents deserved better opportunities. Living in mixed-income neighborhoods populated by healthy working families helps to provide access to such opportunities.

Revitalizing such neighborhoods by turning them into mixed-income places renders them healthier. Similarly, when displaced low-income residents move out of public housing and obtain a voucher that they can use to rent in a mixed-income neighborhood, research demonstrates that such residents are better off.[123] As David Grusky, director of the Center on Poverty and Inequality at Stanford University, put it, when it comes to social mobility, "neighborhoods matter in a really big way." Harvard Professor Nathaniel Hendren adds: "Every extra year of childhood spent in a better neighborhood seems to matter." Data indicates, for example, that low-income boys who grow up in low-income neighborhoods generally earn about 35 percent less than similar low-income children who grow up in the best areas for mobility. For girls, the gap is closer to 25 percent.[124]

How do we surmount the challenge of making mixed-income neighborhoods affordable to low income residents? The best solution lies in providing them government subsidized housing vouchers. Mixed-income neighborhoods help connect all of their residents to the outside world. Such connections are a key to gaining access to opportunity and ensuring families a better life.

ACHIEVING VIBRANCY

Bienville Basin illustrates how one can achieve vibrancy in mixed-income neighborhoods. One must satisfy four requirements:

1. *The right location.* Neighborhoods need to be located near other vibrant neighborhoods.

2. *Well planned, designed, and constructed housing.* People want to live in attractive places that are walkable. They want streets that are connected to the community, not cut off. No one wants to live in an isolated neighborhood with concentrated poverty. That was a huge problem with the old housing projects, which were intentionally walled off from the larger community. Design and construction need to be first class.

3. *Good management and income mix.* Public housing projects converted to mixed-income neighborhoods require the right mix of units. Ideally, a third should be market rate. Members of the workforce—even though they may be less affluent—should occupy a third. The unemployed or under-employed poor should live in the final third. Some members of the final third may have engaged in violent criminal activity or have an emotional instability that renders them unsuitable as tenants. The viability of a mixed-income neighborhood requires screening out those who pose a threat to neighborhood safety or stability. Management must be caring and attentive.

4. *Affordable market rate rents.* Rents for the third of the residents who pay market rate for apartments in a mixed-use community will be less than for similar apartments in a non-mixed used community. This is practical reality. Attracting market rate residents to mixed-income communities requires providing them an incentive, such as lower rental costs. Such residents are crucial to providing neighborhood stability. Not having middle-income residents will produce a neighborhood populated mainly by poor residents who require costly social services and become isolated.

HRI believes that diversity strengthens a neighborhood. Diversity produces a much healthier city than one whose neighborhoods consist entirely of the poor or the rich. Homogeneity in neighborhoods is less likely to produce a vibrant, healthy city. HRI makes a special effort to locate housing for the poor in areas that are not depressed. This work is challenging. Middle or upper income areas fiercely oppose the introduction of low-income residents. HRI's philosophy of well-managed diversity serves everyone. They work with public authorities to provide low-income residents who are displaced from former public housing projects a choice as to where they move. Subsidized rent vouchers finance this option. Development is about more than real estate. Social, economic, political, and environment considerations are equally important and guide their decisions on development.

PROVIDING RESIDENTS A CHOICE

Often missed in the planning and development of mixed-income communities is the voice of the actual customer—the community residents. The president of HRI Management, David Abbenante, observes that "policy makers, advocates, and other well intended groups sometimes press for ideas that they deem serves the best interests of the residents. Bienville Basin as well as River Garden, which revitalized the former St. Thomas Housing Development, illustrate the pitfalls. Too often these are ideas advanced by people that do not live in public housing communities and who have not discussed what the residents themselves prefer."

Says Abbenante: "When the Housing Authority of New Orleans (HANO) tore down the Iberville and other housing developments, massive protests erupted. Things got completely out of hand. Folks chained themselves to City Hall. Yet few if any of these folks had lived in a public housing development or had ever talked to the five hundred folks that were desperate to get out of the developments."

Indeed, when HRI began leasing the affordable elderly high rise at the Marais Apartments—the former Texaco building on Canal Street located adjacent to the Iberville project—about ninety-two residents who had lived in Iberville expressed an initial interest, yet only two chose to move into Marais. "Concerned they were making a mistake," Abbenante recounts, "we reached out to the residents again and asked *why* they did not want to return. The responses that came back were revealing. Some said they had just moved nine months ago and didn't want to move again. Some were living closer to a daughter or grandson and liked being near family. Others said they had a backyard at their new place and were happy at their new location. The important point is that former Iberville residents had a choice and they exercised it. While only two people wanted to return to the Iberville neighborhood, ninety chose to stay where they wanted to live."

HRI's Debbie Taullie adds: "Outside advocates were, we felt, misguided. Why were they opposed to the demolition of segregated housing projects occupied by a population of concentrated poor in places afflicted with crime and social problems? We didn't think that made sense. More crucially, neither did the residents of those places. The former residents did not want to go back. Happily for them, they received a choice voucher. They could still choose to move back to an affordable unit by giving up their voucher."

On the other hand, as Bienville Basin opened, a lot of former residents did plan to return. HRI's philosophy favors revitalizing a site that once housed concentrated poor, offering existing residents a housing choice voucher to move anywhere they choose, and offering them the right to return to the new development. It sees its new developments as highly desirable. They are mixed-income, attractive to the entire community, affordable, and recognize the right of individuals to decide for themselves where and how they prefer to live.

FINANCING CHALLENGES

The financing plan required heavy participation from the city and the state to supplement federal funds provided to the project. HRI obtained over $40 million of federally funded, state-controlled gap-financing for housing by demonstrating that because of Iberville's unique location in the center of downtown New Orleans, its redevelopment would transform entire surrounding neighborhoods. Obtaining state tax credits is a highly competitive process. Different developers make applications to the state to obtain them. The state scores each application and awards the tax credits to the highest scoring applicants. The state was so impressed by the concept of transformational projects that it awarded bonus points in its scoring system for the project it deemed to be transformational. Bienville Basin was a winner in that competition.

THE IBERVILLE WORKING TEAM

An Iberville Working Team was assembled. It took into account the needs, desires, and experiences of the many stakeholders. The team included Iberville residents, the City of New Orleans, the Housing Authority of New Orleans, HRI, McCormack Baron Salazar, Urban Strategies, Inc., and community consultants GCR and The Black Men of Labor, Inc. Their goal was to create a mixed-income, mixed-use community that would also revitalize the surrounding neighborhoods.

Their plan provided for new infrastructure and utilities. It incorporated a preservation strategy to highlight historic structures and spaces. It entailed a phased creation of 705 mixed-income apartments. The first phase renovated ten historic buildings in accordance with U.S. Department of Interior Standards. Another six will be completed in later phases. New construction includes four four-story multi-family buildings and four three-story townhouse buildings. A historic cemetery location is respected and preserved as a community park space.

"Varied local architectural details and scale," HRI's Josh Collen says, "will give the new development the organic feel of a place that has evolved over decades." It will provide nearly three acres of public green space plus "cultural corners" at the historic center of the development. The designers were proud that many mature oak trees were preserved and integrated into the new community. The project creates a new National Register Historic District. A combination of true market rate, workforce, and low-income units in the redeveloped Iberville ensures wide diversity.

HRI's Bienville Basin redevelopment combines a traditional New Orleans aesthetic with interpretations that use modern materials and conveniences for residents. "Porches, stoops, balconies, pedestrian scale structures, and landscaping create a walkable community a few steps from Canal Street and the French Quarter," says HRI architect Gary Meadows. "It offers a new day for residents and a brighter future for New Orleans."

Michael Valentino praises the revitalization. He finds "the architectural look and feeling of the Bienville Basin interesting, appealing, and inviting. From the street it does not give you a sense of how massive it really is. It looks residential, not institutional." He believes it has retained "enough of the original fabric to keep its sense of place in history. Blended with the opening of the street grid, a more stable and productive environment has been created. It will offer a safer and healthier location for former residents and newcomers alike, particularly those associated with the medical district. It will favorably impact all of the perimeter neighborhoods, economically and culturally, and reinvigorate the area with a life and vitality that had been lost. It will restore a vibrant, safe community on the perimeter of the Quarter."

Kurt Weigle has reached the same conclusion. "Bienville Basins is a terrific development. It has strong components of high, middle, and low-income housing. But it is perceived positively. It is perceived as a safe, dynamic and growing part of our city." Weigle stresses that the impact extends well beyond the confines of the development itself. "The positive perception is providing incentives for people to invest. That creates a broader tax base and more jobs. It helps residents by opening up new opportunities for them. It helps Tremé, downtown, the French Quarter, and Mid-City by opening new opportunities for residents there. Really, it helps residents across the city."[125]

LAMBERT BOISSIERE

Former New Orleans City Councilman

Former Councilman Lambert Boissiere is arguably the best mayor New Orleans never had. On the City Council, he earned plaudits across the board, from uptown to downtown, the river to the lake, among blacks, whites, and Hispanics, as well as Republicans and Democrats for his ability to bridge differences. "Lambert has extraordinary ability. He has guts. He was and is universally respected as one of the city's great political leaders," says former state representative and Louisiana Commerce Secretary Ron Faucheux, who has worked with him closely.

Boissiere has had a career-long focus on economic development, bridging racial divides, and working for innovative solutions to the challenge of too many concentrated poor in New Orleans. In 1994, he left the Council to run for mayor. In a historic campaign, he aired television advertising that called for the demolition of crime infested public housing developments. "I thought we should relocate public housing residents to renovated abandoned houses. We had twenty-five thousand of them. We could have given each of them their own home," Boissiere says.

His friend and colleague, former Councilman Mike Early notes that "Lambert is a rare political leader. He is among the few African American or white political leaders who have always enjoyed high popularity among both sets of voters. They love his warmth. They admire his passion and commitment. They respect his honesty and integrity."

"Public housing as it existed in 1994 would today be called a slum landlord property," Boissiere says. "Even then we could have called it that. Three-quarters of the units might be abandoned. It was not safe for residents. It cut them off from city services. It denied them opportunity. It was inhumane. I was determined to relocate people to better housing and better, safer neighborhoods."

At the time, he received a "mixed feeling in black and white neighborhoods. People feared that we might bring a criminal element to their homes, which was not true. We would have matched individuals to places for which they were suitable and would be happy," he says. "We could also have redeveloped the land on which the projects sat into mixed-income, affordable housing and commercial developments."

He praises HRI's work on Iberville and St. Thomas, known respectively as Bienville Basin and River Garden. "HRI's work has revitalized the neighborhoods around St. Thomas by adding retail to the residential. It's not just Wal-Mart, it's the other small retail. That has created walkable, safer neighborhoods."

As to Bienville Basin, he states, "it'll be an anchor towards protecting the French Quarter and revitalizing that whole corridor along Rampart Street and Basin Street to Canal Street. You see the Regional Transportation Authority is adding a new streetcar line from Canal to Elysian Fields. This will revitalize the area down to St. Claude. This will bring a major part of the city that had been left behind into the mainstream of prosperity. HRI's work is enhancing the value of properties in all of these areas and will make the lives of people much better. People will be able to walk to shops along Rampart, walk into the Quarter, walk along Canal Street. HRI redeveloped the Texaco Building—now called the Marais Apartments—for senior citizens. It's bringing commerce to the upper end of Canal Street. It has helped cure a sore spot for the city. The whole Basin Street area is being revitalized due to HRI's involvement."

EX304131
CAT

PET FRIENDLY
ONE WAY
NO PARKING

RAYANA SIBLEY
Resident, Bienville Basin

A homemaker and single mother of three small children, she's especially pleased by the friendly atmosphere of cooperation. "The co-workers make us feel homey. They work together to make us feel comfortable. The people are smiling. They're excited about their new houses. They're just beautiful. I didn't expect HRI could make it so nice. Because of the way I live, it makes me want to get up and thrive more for my children to have a better future. It gives me energy, and I've got a lot of hope."

That Iberville is a mixed-community "is a big plus. Now I feel like I'm living among more people from different races. It feels good to have different cultures from different areas around. We have college students. We're getting to know one another. People get along well. I'm excited."

"We even have a gym," she beams. "I get exercise. I can work out and take out my frustrations whenever I please. It makes me a healthier person and a happier person." She feels it's a good place to raise a family.

She loves living in a tourist area. "I walk to Riverwalk. We can sightsee. The bus lines are right there. The French Quarter is a block away. The Insectarium is a short walk. The stores are there. We have places to eat. We even have a Whole Food store in the area, which lets us eat healthy. When you have kids, that makes a difference."

She's looking for a career. "I'm praying a lot. I'm praying to God to open new doors. I'm focused. I have to be. Any mom of three children feels that way. And I have confidence. And I have high hopes. I'm currently enrolled in school through HANO and HRI, which is funding a customer service school for us. I'd like to be a social worker. I love helping people." She recently graduated and looks forward to a new life with new opportunities.

OPEN YOUR CELEBRATIONS.
NEW LIMITED EDITION HOLIDAY BOTTLES.

LTV Building

Dallas, Tx. 2016

In 1961, architects Harwood K. Smith and Dales Young Foster designed the trend-setting LTV Tower in downtown Dallas. Named for the Ling-Temco-Vought Corporation, which headquartered in it, the building was the first Dallas high-rise to be clad primarily with a curtain wall system. It opened in 1964 as Dallas's fifth tallest building. Tenants included the National Bank of Commerce, Electro-Science investors, and the American Life Insurance Company. A marble and granite pedestrian mall distinguished the ground floor. An innovative motor bank called "Teller Vision" provided an early form of ATM service.[126]

There's a glow in the eyes of HCI Design, Inc., president Gary Meadows as he reflects on the building's history. "Most dramatic is how the exterior look and form of the building engages with Pacific Avenue on the north and Elm Street on the south. The face was covered with 125,000 square feet of dark glass with strips of aluminum molding and contained the world's largest signboard. Thirty windows on each side of twenty-five floors were individually controlled and could spell out different messages. One even had a picture of Big Tex in lights during the State Fair."

The building was sold in 1968 and went through a series of different owners until 2014, when HRI Properties acquired the property to convert it into a Hilton Garden Inn Hotel and Luxury Apartments. HRI saw an opportunity to create vibrancy in downtown Dallas. As architect Chad Cronin put it, "LTV's prominence on the downtown skyline would make it a beacon. Retail shops, restaurants, and nightclubs within walking distance would enliven activity into the late evening. Opening a new hotel would have a dynamic impact in making that happen."

"The concept of transforming the magnificent first floor lobby into a new hotel entry point was a thrill," project manager architect Jim Cloutman says. "By their shape, size, or other features, some buildings naturally lend themselves perfectly to mixed use. LTV was a perfect candidate."

ADAPTIVE REUSE

HRI conducted an $80 million renovation of the LTV building. It is Dallas's first mixed-used hotel and residential complex. Reporter Jack Fink of *CBS News* in Dallas/Ft. Worth highlighted why the project generated enthusiasm. He points to Main Street and Garden Park, where folks like Shelsea Sanchez who work downtown can walk their dogs during their lunch hour. She and her husband can live in the tower and walk to work. "We wanted to live that city lifestyle, we don't have children yet, so it was perfect for us," she told Fink.[127]

Integrating residences and a hotel posed major architectural challenges. Asbestos abatement, renovation of elevators, new heating and air conditioning, and restoring the exterior were essential. The hotel and the residences each needed their own security and elevators. Sloping streets on two sides of the building created access issues. Parking for the upper floors required new vehicle ramps.

"The building was certain to be listed on the National Register of Historic Properties," Jim Cloutman noted. "The Texas Historic Commission had to approve renovation plans. We had to bear that in mind as we designed renovations." Changing the building from primarily businesses and offices to a residential, multi-family building and hotel required rethinking how the building would be serviced.

HRI worked closely with the architectural firm of Merriman Associates/Architects in bringing the tower back to life. The modern style exterior was retained. The first floor hotel lobby connects the hotel to the street to generate more local activity. The cohesive unit design, security, energy efficiency, access to a restaurant, internal parking, location, and strong amenities make the new hotel and apartments attractive to hotel guests and residents.

The hotel has 171 rooms plus two thousand square feet of meeting space. Guests have exclusive access to a fifth floor outdoor deck, swimming pool, and fitness center. Residents have their own deck and pool on the thirty-second floor. They also share a community room and a fitness center.

"We've created a diverse environment for its residents and guests. It stimulates ground floor activity on Elm Street and Pacific Avenue, while strengthening links between Main Street and Pacific Avenue," says HRI President Tom Leonhard. "We've removed more than half a million square feet of empty space from downtown. This redevelopment returns to commerce an abandoned skyscraper that is historically significant. We talk a lot about walkable livability. This new hotel and apartments are an easy walk to shopping, entertainment, and the DART light rail."

John Crawford, the CEO of Downtown Dallas, Inc., has praised the project for "giving our downtown revitalization efforts another boost." He adds that it "serves as yet another example of the importance of public/private partnerships to achieve mutual goals and objectives." Dallas Mayor Mike Rawlings declared that the project "will add greatly to the fun, vibrancy, and quality of life" in the area and "attract more urban residents of all ages, incomes, and backgrounds to downtown and continue to establish it as a vibrant neighborhood." Excited by the growth of downtown Dallas, he praised the vision of the HRI team: "We're going to have a place where people can sense urbanism in a new way for Dallas. . . . People want to touch downtown. They want to be part of a connected environment."[128]

TEXAS
Lakes

The HRI Team

BUILDING A GREAT ORGANIZATION
by Tom Leonhard

In August 1988, I was about to graduate with a finance degree from the University of New Orleans. At the time, I was a headwaiter at Arnaud's, a fine dining restaurant in the French Quarter. It struck me that securing an internship would help improve my resumé. My accounting professor suggested that I contact a colleague who was looking to hire an intern to prepare Department of Housing and Urban Development certified payroll forms. The company name was Historic Restoration, Incorporated, owned by Edward B. Boettner and Pres Kabacoff. At the time, HRI only employed about seven people. I would be number eight.

Over the next twenty-seven years, I grew up as HRI grew. Today the company employs over 2,000 people and operates in sixteen states. Named President in 2001, I am proud to be among the company's leaders. During my tenure, we have experienced many ups and downs, three recessions and two national disasters (9/11 and Hurricane Katrina). Through it all, our desire to do the right thing, build great projects, renew cities, preserve historic buildings, and create a strong organization has enabled the company to achieve great success.

Developing real estate, especially historic buildings in urban cores, ranks among the most challenging and rewarding aspects of the real estate industry. It is not for the faint of heart. Success requires vision, endurance, skill, passion, and most importantly, a great team of professionals. HRI has hired that team. They are passionate about revitalizing cities. Most HRI team members have been with the company for over ten years. Many are nearing the twenty-year mark. In today's economy, this kind of employee loyalty is unheard of.

I believe our management philosophy drives this loyalty. One fundamental element of that philosophy is that HRI hires people of good character who want to be part of a team and are self motivated. Everyone wants to be on a winning team, and they've made HRI a winning company.

A second is that we help employees succeed by placing them in positions that enable them to capitalize on their unique skills and passion. People are wired differently. Human beings like to do things they are naturally good at performing. HRI focuses hard on building a team that consists of the right people who perform the right tasks for their passion, and who are committed to doing the right thing for communities.

A third is mutual respect. Every position in the organization is important, from a maintenance man to the general manager of a hotel. Their success is the company's success. Likewise, their failure is the company's failure. We do not tolerate disrespectful or disruptive behavior. Our high level of respect for one another helps create a positive work environment that fosters teamwork and achievement.

Urban real estate development requires strong teamwork. Each team member brings a unique skill set and perspective, and every HRI employee understands this concept. They work collaboratively to achieve organizational goals even if they have to compromise with other team members. A spirit of cooperation also enables the company to deal with crises and team members to pitch in to solve problems and support other departments within the company.

Personal accountability is another trait that sets the HRI team apart. Mistakes will be made and lessons will be learned. How the company deals with these mistakes sets HRI apart. Intentional errors are not tolerated. The good of the company always trumps the good of the individual employee. HRI's employees recognize the deeply competitive nature of the real estate environment.

Their commitment to excellence makes a vital difference. Our employees recognize that the company pays them for results and not effort. Each employee holds one another to their high performance standard. The result of this collective spirit is a highly effective and profitable organization built on a track record of strong performance and results.

The HRI organization is built to create and operate complex, urban real estate properties nationwide. The company consists of development professionals, design, finance, construction and property management, and government relations. They work together to enable the company to grow by creating irreplaceable real estate assets in urban areas nationwide.

Lacking capital, the company focused on tertiary markets, where cities provided subsidies to encourage revitalization. In April 2014, HRI partnered with Almanac Realty Investors to invest $150 million of capital into the company. This capital infusion afforded the opportunity to target the top 25 Metropolitan Statistical Areas for growth. It also enabled the company to develop larger projects with costs in excess of $50 to $100 million dollars.

Today, HRI competes effectively in these larger markets because of its unique niche capabilities. We manage the adaptive reuse of historic properties. We combine hotel, apartment, and commercial uses into a single project. HRI's hotel and apartment teams find ways to leverage the mix of hotel and apartment uses to increase revenues and lower operational costs through shared service practices. The company can also size the hotel and residential components of the project to best fit the demands of a particular location and market. The company has learned that it must adapt its approach to design, programming, and style to each individual market's needs. This adaptability is one of the company's greatest strengths.

Real life examples of the HRI teamwork and capabilities are discussed elsewhere in this book. Looking ahead, HRI faces a bright future. The demand for revitalizing cities, restoring historic properties, and urban development is very strong. As the company grows, it will face new challenges and obstacles. I am confident that the organizational strength of HRI Properties will enable the company to continue profitable growth in cities around the country.

EDWARD B. BOETTNER: A TRIBUTE
by Brenda Boettner

It was 1980, and I was in my twenties. One day my father asked me to come with him for a ride to see a surprise. I heartily agreed and off we went, heading in the direction of downtown. Unknown to me, we were proceeding into the "skid row" or "no man's land" part of town, and that frightened me. When I expressed my concern, dad told me not to worry. As the car began to slow, I saw an enormous brick building that looked to me like it was about to fall down. The weeds in front were taller than I was. The broken railroad tracks made navigation difficult as we approached the front of the building. Windows were shattered, and smelly debris was everywhere.

As we stood amid this mess, he pronounced, "I am buying this building and going to turn it into luxury apartments." The glowing look in his expression and the excitement in his voice was infectious, and I agreed that this was an excellent idea. On the way home I got my first lesson in historic tax credits as he attempted to explain how the financing was all going to work. At first I did not understand the enormity of the "deal," but over the years I grew to comprehend the risks. Things were never easy. But as Pres Kabacoff has well stated, HRI's journey began with that building—the Federal Fibre Mills.

At the time that Ed and Pres were introduced, they realized that they both lived in Lake Vista. They were perfect business partners. Ed was older, and Pres was a ball of energy. Pres would call the house every morning at dawn and their day would begin—meeting after meeting, on the phone constantly with each other. I had no idea what it would take to start a business like this. What I did know was that the oil bust had left New Orleans's economy in bad shape. That made real estate development a high risk, especially in an area that had seen no residential development in a hundred years. In addition, interest rates were at 16 percent on home loans. Ed's enthusiasm got everyone beyond all of that. He had a vision and knew it would work.

Portrait of Edward B. Boettner by artist Arie Van Selm.

For their first project, Ed and Pres had one employee, Sandy Conroy, a computer whiz who knew construction. There was huge promise for a great World's Fair and terrific publicity for what they had done. They expected immediate success. Alas, things didn't turn out that way. Once the fair ended, the area became neglected and vacant again. But there was a silver lining; the neighborhood infrastructure had been repaired for the fair. It proved the perfect starting point for their new development.

My dad was a salesman with a vibrant personality. He could talk to anyone. After graduating from Loyola in 1954, he and the two Eberts brothers started Century Printing, which later became Century Graphics. Ed became the lead salesman. He told me about the cold calls he had to make, and his anxiety sitting in his car while gathering the courage to enter a prospective client's office. Once he got through the door, he was a natural. Over the next fifteen years, he sold printing to clients all over the country, mostly in the form of newspaper circulars.

A master at entertaining, he often included his wife Donna and his seven children in the process. His house on Swan Street in Lake Vista, with a massive façade and a direct view of Lake Pontchartrain at the rear, was an impressive place to bring clients. They often left feeling like a part of the big family. On many evenings, and until their deaths, my dad liked to visit his parents for dinner. He loved his mother's cooking. His favorite meal was paneed pork chops with mashed potatoes and green beans. My grandmother was always so happy to feed him. After dinner, he would sit in the lounge chair and fall asleep. While he slept, she would whisper to me across the room, worried about his health. She was a worrier by nature but she sensed the stress that his new real estate venture was placing on him. She needn't have. He was unstoppable.

HRI's second historic conversion, the Woodward Wight building, opened in February 1987. Attracting pioneering residents, it presented me with my first job in leasing. From the moment the building opened, the pressure to sign leases was intense. Everyday we planned and implemented our marketing program. The whole thing was a struggle. Indeed, it took about twenty-four months to sign enough residents to secure a permanent loan for the project. We were open seven days a week, and I often took the Sunday shift. After taking my grandma to church on Sunday, my Dad would bring her down to the Woodward Wright and hang out with me in the office. And believe me, that office was something else. It consisted of four walls erected amid a 30,000 square foot open storage space on the first floor. It was furnished with an air conditioner and a desk. It was very comfortable.

On one occasion, a resident walked past the office and I whispered to my grandma, "there is the man I am going to marry!" That caught her by surprise as she was unaware I had a boyfriend. I said that I didn't but that I had just leased to him and was crazy about him. Two years later, I did marry him. There were several successful marriages among residents who met at the Woodward back in the day.

The typical resident was a professional male who worked in the Central Business District. Fearing that nobody wanted to live in old warehouses, my dad launched a campaign to name the area the Historic Riverfront District, but the name Warehouse District stuck and that's how it's still known. We often marketed the property by hosting parties on the rooftop. It's a good thing we were all young then because it was non-stop.

Soon enough, Ed and Pres were on to more. On the Henderson (opened in 1988), they teamed up with partners out of Philadelphia. This 60,000 square foot former sugar warehouse was a breeze compared to the size of the Woodward and the Federal Fibre Mills. Then came St. Mary, which opened in 1989 with 105 apartments.

By now, Ed and Pres had started to hash out the concept of stacking tax credits using historic and low-income credits in combination. With the help of Billy Connick, who had the church connection, they began work on the historic Catholic school Mater Dolorosa. Together they found a way to bring these old school buildings back into commerce. The Mater Dolorosa offers sixty units for elderly poor citizens.

I began to understand another of my father's passions. He was a true advocate for the poor. He saw how investment could improve these blighted neighborhoods. In his words, "charity can not cure poverty but investment could." In that spirit, HRI began venturing into blighted neighborhoods to restore historic school buildings and hospitals.

Ed also started working with Dickie Breaux from Breaux Bridge, Louisiana. They found several properties in smaller cities or towns like Lafayette and New Iberia. HRI converted these into housing for elderly poor. Among Ed's favorites was the conversion of the old New Iberia High School into residential apartments. Its beautiful façade set among the majestic oak trees was an inspiration to him. He worked closely with Tom Leonhard of HRI on these projects. He had mentored Tom since hiring him from an accounting firm in 1988 through the time of Ed's death in May, 2000.

Next Ed and Pres turned their sights to Canal Street, the French Quarter, and the historic Central Business District in New Orleans. They developed the D.H. Holmes Apartments and Chateau Sonesta Hotel—today the Hyatt French Quarter hotel. Gravier Place and later the Hilton Garden Inn French Quarter/CBD built upon those prior successes.

Ed loved the D.H. Holmes apartments—so much so that he decided to live there upon selling the family home in Lake Vista. He took a large apartment that had a balcony facing Bienville. He loved the noise of the quarter, which he could hear from his bedroom through the open balcony doors.

He loved Lucky Dogs! And Kastleburgers!

One evening, he went off to the five-star Arnaud's for dinner. On reaching Bourbon Street, he was drawn to the aroma of a Lucky Dog cart. He looked at the vendor and said aloud in front of a small crowd, "You know, I can't decide. Do I want to go to Arnaud's or take a Lucky Dog?" He thought a moment and continued, "You know, I think I'll take a Lucky Dog." And he did. Realizing that Ed's public pronouncements could increase sales, the vendor pulled him aside and asked if he'd do that more often. It was typical Ed.

Ed travelled in Yellow Cabs from the time he moved downtown. Fortunately he had quit driving, as his driving skills were not that keen. The cab drivers loved him. I don't know exactly why. Perhaps he was a big tipper, perhaps he told good stories—who knows? Nevertheless, when he was lying in a coma in the hospital, the cab drivers held a prayer vigil for him at their headquarters. When he died, they offered to transport the family from the funeral home to the church and back. I remember riding in the taxi with my two young boys and a cousin. As we were driving down Poydras as part of the funeral

Boettner Park, heart of the River Garden development, New Orleans, La.

process, my son said "Mom, look at all those people staring at us. Grand dad must have been a pretty important man. Look at all the yellow cabs!"

The Cotton Mill was among the grandest of the warehouses in the district. For many years it was underutilized and vacant. We spent many days walking through the empty warehouse looking at its potential. Ed had imagination. I was so fortunate to learn from him!

The Cotton Mill was the largest residential development undertaken by HRI at the time. It's just gorgeous. I remember the grand opening ceremony like it was yesterday. And I loved Ed talking about how he'd climb into the base of the old masonry chimney located in the courtyard. He said that the base of it was all nicely padded. A candle on the wall provided the sole illumination. He could go in there with a bottle of wine and a lady friend and listen to the sounds of the wind blowing over the top of the chimney. "What a magical experience and what an amenity!" he'd exclaim.

I left HRI in 1998 and did not return until 2002. As that time went by, dad kept me up to date on HRI matters. Things were still stressful. Among his projects, revitalizing the St. Thomas housing development stirred his biggest passion. Ed and Pres pushed for ten years to get the St. Thomas project/Hope VI going. Ed worked closely with the St. Thomas residents' council. Amazingly, they loved him despite hating, as they saw it, the idea of rich developers bent on tearing down their housing. Fannie McKnight was a leader among the residents and a very formidable woman with a temper for those she felt failed to stand up for the residents. But Ed won her over. She even wrote a poem that she delivered at his funeral. I was proud to read it at his gravesite. It was a beautiful description of their friendship.

Ed had departed this life by the time River Garden was developed but we look to him as its inspiration. It was in some ways the emblem of his life's work. He had a passion to help the less fortunate, and his spirit shined on them. He had enormous generosity. He did not ask for much. He did not require much. He was a simple man and in his later years expressed his desire to be humble.

I think he achieved that.

He is remembered today at "Boettner Park" which is located in the heart of River Garden.

Brenda Boettner is the daughter of HRI Properties Co-Founder Edward B. Boettner, and one of company's longest tenured employees.

PRES KABACOFF

Co-Founder & Executive Chairman of the Board, HRI Properties

Tall, slender, athletic, wearing his trademark goatee beard and dressed neatly in business casual clothes, the Chief Executive Officer combines a gentle man with a powerful intellect and relentless energy. Pres Kabacoff is an idealist who feels deeply and passionately about his work and the civic causes for which he provides leadership. He champions the revitalization of historic buildings with fervor. His understanding of real estate development built upon public-private partnerships and how development can transcend the merits of a particular project and benefit surrounding neighborhoods has earned him a national reputation in his industry.

His father, Lester Kabacoff, was a leading developer in New Orleans who led the revitalization of the city's riverfront, the New Orleans Hilton Riverside and Towers, the Riverwalk, the International Cruise Ship Terminal, and the Beau Chene recreational community in St. Tammany Parish. His mother, Gloria, was renowned for her charm and civic activism in the arts and other activities. "Both had an important influence in my life," says Kabacoff, who also singles out Julius Rosenwald, the owner of Sears Roebuck. "Julius financed five thousand schools for African American children. He showed great courage and the difference that an individual can make. My dad had worked closely with Edith Stern, the daughter of Julius. The fact is, he and his family had a great influence on ours."

A graduate of the University of Denver and LSU Law School, he practiced law for ten years then moved into real estate. "My dad was developing Beau Chene and the Hilton Hotel. These were the most significant real estate projects happening in the state. I wanted to be a part of it."

The experience led to his co-founding HRI Properties, Inc., in New Orleans with Edward B. Boettner in 1982. HRI is a full service real estate company and a leader in the adaptive reuse of historic structures. Its mission statement is to revitalize cities by creating diverse, vibrant, and sustainable communities. "I've done everything I know how to keep the company true to that mission statement," he declares. "And we've done so."

Kabacoff's civic activities read like an encyclopedia of community service. Working with Chris Johnsen of the Young Leadership Council, he was a leader in the movement that led to the lighting of the Mississippi River Bridge and the installation of the Riverfront streetcar. "Lighting the bridge was a way to symbolize the importance of the river," he says. The lights became a symbol after Katrina, forming the background image for national news reporting.

Kabacoff worked to reintroduce the Riverfront streetcar line into the city. At one time the city had six hundred miles of streetcars. He provided leadership as well that has led to reinstalling the Rampart/St. Claude line (originally called the Desire line), which will reinstall Tennessee Williams's storied streetcar named Desire. "We needed to reverse the foolish decision to remove six hundred miles of streetcar tracks, which removed attractive public access to every point of the city. There was a belief that the car and bus could answer our transportation needs. It was misguided."

One of New Orleans's most dynamic civic leader, the posts he has held attest to his community commitment. He chaired the mayor of New Orleans's Housing Task Force Committee for Mitch Landrieu. He's been active in the Urban Land Institute, which works to provide responsible leadership for land use to enhance the total environment. He chairs the Development Committee of the LOCUS Organization, which consists of the leading real estate developers in the nation. He has also served as an advisory board member of the Brookings Institute's Center for Urban and Metropolitan Policy. He's one of 250 trustees of the Committee for Economic Development, a national research and education organization that seeks solutions to pressing social and economic issues. He's a member of the National Advisory Council of the Trust for Public Land, a national non-profit land conservation organization. He has served as a member of the Orleans Parish School Board and on the Boards of Dillard University, the Public Affairs Research Council of Louisiana, the New Orleans Police Foundation, Smart on Crime, and the governor's NFL Stadium Advisory Commission. "I don't jump on every civic cause. I jump in where I feel I can make a difference. Then it becomes a calling," he explains.

He is the recipient of many honors. These include the 1989 First Citizen of the Learning Society, a business/education award presented by the University of New Orleans Council for Lifelong Learning; one of five individual Peacemakers' awards by the New Orleans Peace Foundation for his love and dedication to the City of New Orleans, and the National Council of Jewish Women (NCJW) Greater New Orleans Section's prestigious Hannah G. Solomon Award (Founder). He has also received an honorary doctorate of humanities from the University of New Orleans.

Kabacoff hopes to be remembered "as a fellow who combined his social work and business efforts to create a positive, enduring impact on communities."

EDDIE BOETTNER

Chief Administrative Officer & Board Member, HRI Properties

Even before Eddie Boettner joined HRI Properties, he was a proven entrepreneur whose energy and drive had made him a standout success. Graduating from Rochester Institute of Technology in printing management, he wasn't the type to send job applications. Instead he started his own publishing company, *News on Wheels*. The publication listed used vehicles, trucks, and boats for sale. The idea epitomized Boettner's bottom-line, pragmatic approach to business. "It was successful. I had seen a copy of an auto trader from another part of the country," he recalls. "I said there's nothing like this in New Orleans. I know how to do this. And it will be easy. I was right on the first two. But it wasn't easy."

In 1989, he sold the publication to a division of the *Milwaukee Journal*. He worked there for another ten years. "I continued to build publications in New Orleans and beyond. I enjoyed building the printing business and did so for the *Journal* until 1998." After a brief try at retirement, Boettner spoke to Pres Kabacoff about joining HRI.

"My wife wanted me out of the house, and I had built a multi-million dollar enterprise. I warned Pres I knew nothing about real estate," he recalls. Pres was unfazed by Boettner's trademark measured approach. "No problem," Kabacoff told him. "You are an entrepreneur. You built a multi-million dollar company. We'll teach you real estate." The deal was sealed. Boettner joined HRI Properties and works in site acquisitions, looking for new projects.

"It was an introduction to more and more of what we do around here," he observed. When his father and Kabacoff's partner, Edward B. Boettner, passed away in 2000, he took on the responsibilities of chief administrative officer. He relishes his responsibilities. "My role gives me the opportunity to influence the way we operate. I have a say in the organization and direction of the company." What strikes him the most about the company is its "unique ability to take defunct buildings, like old bank buildings, and repurpose them. We give buildings that would never have continued to exist new life. We breathe new life and vitality into the neighborhoods and cities."

Respected at HRI for his low-key, disciplined, orderly thinking, Boettner stresses teamwork as a key to the success of any business. That's especially important at HRI, which now employs 2,000 people. He's especially keen on recruiting millennials. "I take a lot of satisfaction from working with an energetic group of young men and women who are as passionate about their work as I am. Their energy is infectious."

What does he hope for as he peers over the horizon? "I'd like to see my children and grandchildren nurture and develop the same feelings as I have for our history, our culture, our built environment. I want to know that HRI is a lasting organization. I've helped create its foundations. I want to see HRI live long beyond myself. In short, I'd rather have helped build a clock than tell time," he says, smiling. "That spirit carries through the entire organization. We are clock builders, not time tellers. HRI will survive all of us. We have built a good organization that will thrive and prosper long after I'm gone."

TOM LEONHARD

President & CEO, HRI Properties

Born at Hotel Dieu in New Orleans, HRI President Tom Leonhard is the next generation leader of a company that is expanding into a national powerhouse. Soft-spoken and good-natured, his warm personal style epitomizes HRI's culture. Coats and ties are eschewed in favor of business casual. Everyone from the top down works with open doors and everyone enjoys easy access to one another. It fosters the team spirit that Leonhard prizes.

Leonhard graduated from Jesuit High in New Orleans and went on to obtain a degree in finance and an MBA at UNO, where his father, a professor, taught political science. "I received an excellent education," he recounts, "but that was secondary. During one class, I met my wife."

He's quick to relay the lore that pervades HRI that has him doing an early stint as a waiter at Arnaud's. "I was a captain," he notes, setting the record straight, and laughs, "People worked for me." He enjoyed the experience and learned from it. "I was good at it. What I loved was you work hard, get paid, go home and you never think about it until the next shift. The fact was, though, I wanted to be waited on, not to be the waiter. The job was eye-opening." Arnaud's attracts the business community. "I'd talk to business people," he recalls, "and they told me about what they did, asked me about myself, and I realized that what I most wanted to do was business."

What motivated him to join HRI? "I was impressed with Ed Boettner and Pres Kabacoff and the work the company was doing. I thought it was exciting to renovate an old warehouse into a place where people could live. I actually moved into the St. Mary's apartments in the Warehouse District after I graduated from college. I joined as a payroll clerk. I did certified payrolls that HUD required for construction projects."

HRI has proven an ideal home for Leonhard. His financial acumen, skill in managing people, and proficiency in handling negotiations has earned him a place in the first rank of New Orleans business leaders. That's partly because he's open to trying new ideas and encouraging colleagues to join him in making things happen. It was a trait that manifested itself early on.

Leonhard likes to recall how after he joined HRI, Pres Kabacoff expressed a desire to learn more about balance sheets. "Pres was always asking me about pro formas," he recounts. "I told him, look, Wade Ragas is teaching this finance course at UNO. It's a graduate level course. Come audit the course with me. I'll talk to Wade and get his OK. Pres was game, so I went to Wade, who said fine and that's exactly what we did. I was twenty-four years old. Pres was twice my age. Wade taught us both a lot about finance."

His hard work and energy has proven a boon to the company, and as president he's the heir apparent to Pres. Hard-working and enthusiastic, he thinks and dreams big. But people, not ambition, matter most to him. "What's most important to me is that we've got a company where people love to work, where our work is respected by everyone, where an affiliation with HRI properties is a positive experience," he says.

Like other HRI executives, he places great emphasis on his faith and family. "My wife and children come before everything else. Friends are important. They're like family. And that's the perspective that I bring as president. We treat the people we work with as family. We love talented, smart, motivated people who can contribute."

Not surprisingly, Leonhard sets high goals and expects the HRI team to meet them. "We want talented people who possess the highest ethical standards: people who are honest, who are always committed to the right thing, even if

it's the wrong thing for the company. And that's really been the magic of the company. We always make sure when a decision is made that we ask: Is it the right thing to do? If it's not, we'll do [it right] even if it costs us."

He can be a hard-nosed negotiator when putting together deals, but the trust he inspires inside and outside of HRI is well known. His warmth and idealism are apparent. "HRI is a very distinctive company. Obviously the bottom line is critical and our business model has proven enormously successful. But what sets us apart is that while achieving financial success, we strive to carry out our mission of making the lives of others and our community better. I want to help New Orleans to be the city it aspires to be," he says.

As he reflects on the arc of his career, Leonhard feels pride and a sense of fulfillment even as he keeps his eye fixed firmly on the direction for the future in which he is leading HRI. "It's hard to believe I've been with the company twenty-seven years. I wonder where the time has gone. And I'm only forty-eight. I've spent half my time with the company. Not many people can say that in America."

DAVID ABBENANTE

President, HRI Management

David was born in Biloxi, Mississippi, or, as he says, "back east." At HRI, he's the go-to-guy for managing HRI's diverse portfolio of apartments. He holds the title of President, HRI Management, which bears stewardship over these properties. "My role is to make each resident feel like their apartment is their home. We offer a place where people feel comfortable, surrounded by friends, neighborhoods, and places you want to be."

A graduate of the University of Southern Mississippi in business, he joined HRI in the late 1990s to learn the development business. "My first project was developing artist housing in Hammond, Louisiana. It came in on time, under budget, and achieved every operating projection. I was proud of what our team achieved. More important, I was proud of the positive impact it had on downtown Hammond. We took a vacant, blighted school building and converted it into twenty-eight vibrant apartment lofts for artists. They live there, work there, and utilize the historic auditorium to showcase their work.

"I love working at HRI. It's committed to its mission. We have a culture that animates all of our work. That culture is rooted in the precept that we can make a difference in people's lives. We create wonderful spaces. We bring in businesses that serve residents. We offer a lifestyle for folks at every end of the spectrum. We serve those with low incomes who need affordable housing. We serve the more affluent, who can afford to pay market-rate. We purchase the work of our artists who live in residence to enliven common spaces. I find that immensely satisfying because ultimately, what we are creating are communities within communities."

Family lies at the core of his values. "At HRI we work hard because we like what we do. But we put families first." Abbenante is married and takes pride in his two teenage children, Mia and Ethan. He has high hopes for their future. "I want to see them achieve their high potential, which I see as unlimited. I want them to do what brings them happiness and helps their community. Making a difference in the community in which they live and the lives of those around them is very important."

Nothing illustrates David Abbenante at HRI better than his ability to listen to residents and to satisfy their requests. "This business is not about mortar and bricks. It's about people. As long as you keep that top of mind, you know things are going to work out."

DEBBIE TAULLIE

Director of Operations, HRI Management

Debra Taullie is the team leader, mentor, and motivator in directing the day-to-day operations for the apartments that HRI manages. "Every day presents a new challenge," she says. "When your responsibility includes providing quality housing for thousands of people in numerous cities, your days are filled with managing tasks from the ordinary to the extraordinary."

She loves her work. "A great deal of it involves problem solving, decision making, and guiding others to perform," she states. "It takes energy and hard work, but the results pay off because we work hard at creating a positive atmosphere that motivates people."

Debra joined HRI in 2008. She had held senior management positions for two national firms, Johnstown American Companies and Pilot Property Company, prior to joining HRI. There she supervised properties ranging from luxury apartments in upscale markets to affordable and distressed housing and commercial properties—all in over twenty-seven states.

"At Johnstown, the company's motto was 'Make it happen,'" she explains. "That's a work ethic I've maintained. I try to figure out what it takes to get the job done." Her energy is a quality she's had since youth. As a full time honor student, she raised her two younger brothers and helped nurse her mother during a lengthy, terminal illness that took her life at age forty. "The experience made me a better person. It taught me to combine strength and empathy. I learned that almost anything can be accomplished. You just need the desire, dedication, and [to] follow through."

She enjoyed Pilot for its innovative approaches. "Pilot asked themselves, 'how can we be unique and stand apart?'" One key lay in studying other industries and understanding how they became successful. Her team coined the phrase "piggyback marketing" and "saturation marketing." Piggyback marketing meant adapting marketing strategies from other industries, such as fast food or retail chains and applying them to the real estate industry. Saturation marketing ensures maximizing opportunities to publicize properties. "We created a campaign we called Pi-latto. It involved a lottery type sweepstakes to entice new renters and retain existing residents. The campaign drew national attention and was hugely successful," she says.

At HRI, her energy and talent is on full display. "HRI had developed phenomenal historical properties. Managing the HRI portfolio is exciting. I'm a glass half-full person.

"The first project I managed for HRI was American Can in Mid-City. The city's rental occupancy was experiencing a slump. But it was evident that we could make it out-perform the market. American Can's architecture and aesthetics were awesome. We used 'out of the box' ideas to market the property. Our team quickly filled up the property, increased revenues, and out-performed the market."

She's also proud of HRI's mission to improve communities and the company's ability to provide housing for residents of all income levels. "As the director, most complaints and obstacles wind up on my desk. That gives me the opportunity to make a difference. We help people move from homelessness into apartment dwellers. We transform dying buildings into vibrant communities."

As a former national trainer and marketing director, she finds it rewarding to forge a team of employees driven to achieve. "During Hurricane Isaac many were evacuating. We knew that many seniors in our buildings would not evacuate. They would lack food or power. We stepped into high gear, bringing them water, food, and supplies and making sure our buildings remained safe. Residents appreciated our efforts, as so many had no other family or friends to assist."

She doesn't flinch about what she views as her greatest achievement. "For me," she beams, "it's my son. I'm extremely proud to know that I've raised one of the city's brightest and honorable young men. Soon he'll be graduating with his doctorate in nurse anesthesiology. His career choice has involved dedication to saving others' lives. I think it's a wonderful thing he's doing."

GARY MEADOWS

President, HCI Design, Inc.

Another HRI New Orleans-born and bred native (except for an excursion to Baton Rouge for five years where he studied architecture), Gary Meadows has planted his feet firmly on the Crescent City's soil. He loved LSU. "I thought it was fantastic," he says. "The program and professors were terrific and a lot of high school friends were attending. It was also great to be close to New Orleans so that I could maintain ties to friends and family here. I was one of the fortunate ones who was required to work during college and that work was in New Orleans. I worked in my family's residential construction business.

"My dad and two brothers were residential contractors. I grew up with construction in my blood. My grandfather was [a] lumber and timber man. That was in my blood. After graduating, I talked to my father to seek his advice for a career choice. He suggested I get involved with companies that engage in design-build." Such companies combine contracting with architectural services. "I worked with Woodward Design + Build and Broadmoor Design, which was affiliated with Broadmoor Construction and the Boh Corporation."

His coming to HRI was a story in itself. While at Broadmoor, he was second-in-command to Dean Duplantier, with whom he had also worked at Woodward. HRI was converting D.H. Holmes Department Store into apartments and a hotel. "I worked on the hotel," he notes. "This was my first hotel. We worked closely with the general manager and assistant general manager at the Royal Sonesta Corporation, which was going to run the new hotel, to be called Chateau Sonesta. They knew everything about the business and were generous in sharing information.

"Holmes was really interesting. It was a hospitality project that converted a hundred year-old department store into a hotel. We made the first site visit to the building and were greeted by a rush of water flooding out of the exterior doors on the street. What had happened was that this coincided with the time that the city had three days of freezing weather. The sprinkler lines had frozen and then burst. Since the building was vacant, it could flow freely into the building, soaking and ruining the beautiful old wood floors, which buckled.

"The key architectural challenge was that the store wasn't one building. It started as one small structure, and as years passed, Holmes annexed and added on additional buildings. None of the floors lined up. There were many different types of construction. There was literally a town house buried in the middle of the store, on the Bourbon Street side, used for storage. It had been shut off fifty years prior. It was like a snapshot in time."

Meadows designed a renovation that connected the different parts of the hotel so that they flowed smoothly. "We had to change floor elevations in ways that guests did not realize they were walking through multiple buildings. There was an interesting element to the exterior. To qualify for historic tax credits, the 1960s alterations had to be removed. We thought that they had built it over the historic terra cotta façade. Actually they had hammered the façade away. We had to replicate the façade on Canal Street in order to qualify the entire building for historic tax credits.

"We found a unique small sub-contractor who was really an artisan. He created clay molds that served as forms to replicate the façade in fiberglass." He found the process amazing. The sixty-five-foot façade on Canal Street is fiberglass. "And in the twenty-plus years since it was constructed, little maintenance has been required. That's been very pleasing.

"In designing and building this hotel, HRI expressed an interest in developing an in-house capacity for architectural design. In the past, HRI had worked with different architects on their multi-family projects. They felt they had to spend a lot of time explaining to the architects what they wanted and that it made sense to develop their own in-house capability. An HRI executive, Chuck Rutledge, recruited me for HRI."

The offer caught Meadows off-guard. "I thought I had the best job in the world at Broadmoor. But Rutledge was persuasive. I went to a meeting at HRI and at the start thought to myself, 'Heavens, I hope they don't ask me to go to work for them.' By the end of it, I was hoping they would." And they did. "It turned out to be the best career choice in my life."

JOSH COLLEN

Vice President, Development, HRI Properties

I grew up outside of Chicago, about twenty minutes past O'Hare airport, not too far away from what was at the time the largest shopping mall in America. I think of it as a "generic" American suburb. We took family and/or field trips into Chicago every other month growing up. Great city, but I can't really say I'm from Chicago.

I became interested in architecture and city planning even before college. I had an internship at an architecture firm outside Chicago working the blueprint machine in a small, enclosed space. I found myself looking for other options. A social studies teacher told me about city planning.

That led to an internship in the planning department of the city of Hoffman Estates. I had a cool project. Sears was moving from their famous downtown tower to the suburbs. I worked on the requirements for restoration of prairie lands and landscaping around the new Sears building. It was all interesting.

At the University of Illinois, Champaign-Urbana, I studied city and regional planning. I went on to obtain a masters from Cornell. Ironically, even by that age, I had yet to live in a large city. Cornell is located in Ithaca, New York. It's a city, but not a large one. When I studied real world city issues, I found myself in Rochester, where I immersed myself in affordable housing and community development issues. At the same time, I was also a teaching assistant for real estate classes at Cornell.

Cornell was intellectually stimulating with amazing professors who were masters of their topics—land use, historic preservation, and regional planning metrics. My colleagues were equally impressive. Most already had a lot of work experience. On graduation, I went looking for the right city and the right job. It was time to get into practice. I looked in Boston, New York, and Washington, D.C. The best opportunity turned out to be with the AFL-CIO Housing & Building Investment Trusts. I worked in D.C. with them as a financial analyst for a year and a half.

I wanted to do community development real estate work in the trenches, so I joined the Community Development & Preservation Corporation. Also located in D.C., it let me work on two amazing, large-scale projects. One was a complicated public housing high-rise redevelopment, and the other, a set of three historic apartment buildings overlooking the nation's capital. I gained exposure to the complexity of development and the concept that projects were your children.

The Michaels Development Company outside of Philadelphia was my next stop. As a Vice President of Development I had charge of two large-scale mixed-income redevelopments of failed public housing projects. One was located in Tampa, the other was the Desire Housing Project in New Orleans. In 2001, I moved to New Orleans to manage this work.

I fell in love with the city and my lovely New Orleans-born and bred bride. While working on Desire, I watched HRI accomplish amazing things in redeveloping the St. Thomas development. After Katrina, seeing the incredible opportunity to work on a diverse pipeline of projects that would preserve the city's history and launch its recovery, I reached out to HRI. They took me on and threw me into the deep end on three challenging projects. Each was quite distinct: adaptive reuse artist lofts, restoration of senior housing, and a new construction mixed-income project in the Warehouse District.

I quickly learned that a great deal could be accomplished at HRI thanks to the culture of close teamwork and the exceptional ability of my colleagues. What I find most exciting is getting results. This is a company that gets results. The results are meaningful for the neighborhoods, cities, and customers.

This job can be an emotional roller coaster. When you're facing steep challenges that change on a daily basis and evolve constantly, and you're emotionally committed to your projects, you tend to feel every step forward or back. For example, negotiating an extension of a long-term lease with an order of priests that wanted to take back possession of their buildings can be a drawn out affair, which is especially challenging when time is of the essence. You're emotionally committed to making your project happen. They're just as emotional in their understandable desire to protect the interests of their order.

When we did 225 Baronne, there was an obvious challenge. How could we persuade the National Park Service to individually list the building on the National Register of Historic Places? The challenge was the building didn't pass muster based on its architectural significance or as the work of a master of design. We got past that by conducting extensive research into the building's prominent role in advancing the city's Central Business District. I found managing the team that solved the problem fulfilling.

What matters most to me is my family. I want them to be happy, healthy, and we always want to expose our son to exciting new learning experiences. I want to create. I want to be responsible for creating incredible places. I want to be part of building a great company. I love my work. Along with my family, it defines my identity.

STEVE NANCE

Vice President, Investment, HRI Properties

Steve Nance manages the debt and joint venture equity relationships for HRI. He is also the project executive on select projects. His personality is well illustrated by the story he tells about providing an update to CEO Pres Kabacoff. The incurably optimistic Kabacoff had wanted to know the status of HRI's efforts to find distressed hotels and the money to buy and fix them up. Born with a dry sense of humor, Nance grinned and said "I have good news and bad news. I have identified lots of distressed hotel opportunities. The bad news, we already own all of them." That was in 2008, in depths of a deep national—some would say worldwide—recession. The efforts of energetic executives like Nance has ensured that HRI has survived and prospered.

Born in New Orleans, he graduated from LSU in petroleum land management, focusing on business and real estate, and went on to earn an MBA from the University of New Orleans. He came to HRI after fifteen years in commercial banking at J.P. Morgan Chase and Hibernia National Bank. "My time in banking taught me how to finance projects and companies. I've been doing that my whole career. When working with bankers it helps to understand where they are coming from and matching the bank's objectives with the financing needs of the project. I help our team understand how bankers think and how to tackle HRI's banking needs," he says.

His career at HRI kicked off with the Hyatt Place Convention Center. Originally a Holiday Inn that was family-owned, it enjoyed a terrific location but was poorly run. HRI was asked to look at managing the hotel, which quickly turned into an opportunity to acquire the property. HRI, along with two new equity partners, purchased the hotel and worked with Berkadia, who served as the lender, to restructure the hotel's debt. HRI secured a Hyatt Place franchise, renovated the hotel top to bottom, and a year later opened it as the first Hyatt Place in New Orleans. "What we figured out was that we could put together complicated deals on distressed hotels and attract the private equity partners we needed," says Nance. "What we learned was that a better idea was funding our own capital and owning 100 percent of these properties, so we began working towards that goal."

Up next came the Hyatt French Quarter. Originally the Chateau Sonesta (HRI's first hotel project), the hotel needed a new franchise agreement, new debt, new equity partners, a new lease—a whole do-over. "In a difficult hotel market that suffered from the post-Hurricane Katrina effects and a worldwide recession, the relationships I had developed enabled HRI to bring in a new of set of debt and equity partners. The equity partners that believed in HRI's business plan have been handsomely rewarded and have completed several follow-on hotel opportunities with HRI since closing on the Hyatt French Quarter deal."

During 2012, he acted as project executive for the LTV Tower project in Dallas, once the world headquarters for Ling-Temco-Vought, a 1960s conglomerate based in Dallas. "We worked with an individual developer who needed additional financing to finish the project that his struggling lender, First National Bank of McCallen, was not able to provide. First National, whom the FDIC wound up seizing prior to HRI acquiring the asset, turned out to be the largest bank failure since the S&L bail-out crisis of the 1980s. The bank had lent tens of millions into the project and still had millions left to go, but was under the watchful eye of the FDIC. The city of Dallas wanted to get the LTV Tower back into commerce. The city had made $26 million of subsidy available to support the project and had nothing but a gutted empty building. After the bank's takeover by the FDIC, HRI and the city turned to the bank regulators to strike a deal that would pay off the bank's loan in full over time and allow HRI to put new financing on the building."

In the crucial meeting, the city took a hard line with the regulators in asking the FDIC to support the HRI proposal. Says Nance, "Acting through representatives of the city department of economic development, the city bluntly advised the regulators that 'their $26 million subsidy was available to HRI because it liked HRI's track record.' The regulators quickly accepted the suggestion and the project went forward."

"We had completed several mixed-use projects before," Nance says. "But this was one of the largest ones the company had done. It was a thirty-two-story office building that we were turning into a hotel and apartments. Downtown Dallas was problematic when it came to finding financing. Texas had a history of over-building. Lenders and investors were wary. We secured a Hilton Garden Inn franchise and fostered in a state historic tax credit program in Texas. With these changes, we were able to finance the project."

Downtown Dallas was experiencing a renaissance. The LTV project helped advance the development of the urban core, connecting downtown Dallas to the high-end uptown part of the city. "As part of the project's financing, HRI was introduced to Almanac Realty Partners in New York, a private equity fund. Almanac liked what it saw in the project and in HRI in general. Almanac invested $150 million in HRI corporately, which allowed HRI to finance LTV and other projects. Through the LTV project, HRI was able to find an equity investor that believed in the management team allowing the company to achieve its goal of attracting its own capital." Today, that capital has propelled HRI from a company with a few hundred million of assets to one that should have over a billion dollars of assets in the near future.

GARY GUTIERREZ

President, HRI Lodging

Gary Gutierrez is President of HRI's lodging division. "I love the hotel business," he says, "and I've dedicated my career to it. I was drawn to the company's unique capability to design, build, and operate properties many consider too difficult to salvage or to manage." His experience is focused on saving historic properties. "For me, customers find an emotional attachment to these unique buildings. Generations of their families often visited these properties to work, play, and live."

He joined HRI after serving as Vice President of Operations at Highgate Hotels, a leading independent hospitality management firm. His skill in forging and executing strategies to turn around distressed hotel properties made him an ideal fit for HRI's approach.

"When we add a hotel to our portfolio," he observed, "whether it is branded by associating with an established hotel name like Hyatt, Hilton or Marriott, or an independent-operated hotel, our focus is on providing excellent customer service and taking care of the associates that serve them."

What excites him? Gutierrez smiles when that question is posed. "I started my hospitality career as a bellman over thirty years ago. Serving people is part of my DNA. HRI offers opportunities for growth and stands apart for that."

SIDNEY BARTHELEMY

Vice President, Government Relations, HRI Properties

The first quality about former Mayor Sidney Barthelemy that comes to the mind of those who know him well is neither his service as mayor of New Orleans nor his current tenure as Vice President for Governmental Relations; it's that he spent seven full years in a Josephite Seminary—the Society of St. Joseph. There's a spiritual quality that he brings to his work in his pastoral, hands-on approach that focuses on each individual. At its heart, government affairs is about understanding what motivates people and identifying creative ways to persuade strong-minded folks with different opinions to find common ground.

As mayor, he followed the city's first African American to hold that office, Dutch Morial. Barthelemy faced stiff opposition in his bid for the job. His warmth and collegiality paved the way for winning and for a well-recognized record of service as mayor. "I believe in helping people. I believe that we are charged with a duty to make the lives of citizens better. I believe in finding ways to generate opportunity for people and creatively funding government besides saddling people with new tax burdens."

He brought these qualities to HRI after winning re-election and serving two terms. "I loved developing projects and building an economic infrastructure. As mayor, I had led the way for the new aquarium, the land-based casino, and the basketball arena. HRI was about developing inner cities. They took abandoned historic buildings and made them economically feasible again. When Pres Kabacoff offered me the opportunity to do what I do best, but in the private sector, I was thrilled and jumped at the opportunity."

Working with government presents complex challenges. "My experience gave me a clear understanding of how government works and how to get things done. You need to know government's needs and how the private sector can meet those needs. People have to trust you—indeed, trust is number one. You have to be transparent. A company like HRI, which touches the lives of so many individuals, needs to show that its work really does benefit the city and the community. The public official needs to know that a project benefits the city and its people, not just the developer. Earning the trust of public officials depends upon the ability to earn the trust of those whose lives you affect."

The former mayor feels that perspective is the key to success. He was uniquely effective in persuading people—from Governor Edwin Edwards to St. Louis Mayor Clarence Harmon—to see the merit in difficult-to-accomplish projects. In St. Louis, he painted a vision of how a blighted city's downtown could experience a renaissance. With Edwards, he achieved the coordinated effort required to make the casino a reality and the basketball arena available to a National Basketball Association team. It was no accident that the Hornets (today called the Pelicans) came to New Orleans.

At HRI, he gets excited at the focus that HRI has given and the results it achieves in revitalizing historic properties. "It means creating a viable neighborhood in downtowns that were run down and vacant. It means bringing fresh hope to an old city. It means finding that one project that will act as a catalyst to revitalizing whole neighborhoods. We did this in New Orleans, Jackson, Richmond, St. Louis, Winston-Salem. We'll keep doing it across the country. And for our efforts, we'll leave behind better places to live, work, and raise families."

NOTES

1 See, e.g., T.R. Goldman, "The Suburb That Tried to Kill the Car," *Politico Magazine*, October 24, 2015: http://www.politico.com/magazine/story/2015/10/evanston-illinois-what- works-213282?o=2.

2 See, "The Walkup Wake-up Call: Boston," http://www.smartgrowthamerica.org/locus/walkup-boston.

3 Ibid.

4 Applying Boston's walkability ratio to our headquarters city, New Orleans, shows the latter is a long way from satisfying this demand. With a metropolitan population of 1.1mm, New Orleans has added only two new walkable communities in the last twenty-five years—the Warehouse District and the historic Central Business District (CBD). Arguably, the Marigny, and Bywater neighborhoods qualify as walkable communities.

5 Author's interview with Kurt Weigle, October 20, 2015.

6 The legacy company is Historic Restoration, Incorporated. In 2013, the company underwent reorganization. The current name is HRI Properties, LLC. The legacy company handles affordable housing projects. HRI Properties, Inc., handles everything else. For convenience, both companies are referred to in this book simply as HRI. The ownership and management of both companies is identical.

7 Interview with Patty Gay, October 10, 2013.

8 For a Category 1 World's Fair, different nations build their own pavilions. Examples would be the World Fairs held in Chicago (1933) New York (1964), and Montreal (1967). A category 2 Fair places the responsibility upon the host city to build out the premises.

9 Dr. Timothy P. Ryan, "Economic Impact of HRI Properties (HRI) on the New Orleans and Louisiana Economies," September 2012, p. 13.

10 By 2005, when Katrina hit the city, the population had declined to 460,000.

11 Moses was a legendary figure in New York politics. Robert Caro won a Pulitzer Prize for his extraordinary biography of him, *The Power Broker: Robert Moses and the Fall of New York* (New York: Vintage, 1975).

12 Author's interview with Bill Borah, October 20, 2015. See also: William E. Borah and Richard O. Baumbach, Jr., *The Second Battle of New Orleans: A History of the Riverfront Expressway Controversy* (Tuscalossa: University of Alabama Press, 1980)

13 Most older cities have three areas: a historic area; a business district; and a warehouse/transportation district. New Orleans stands apart because of the architecture and close proximity that characterize each of these districts.

14 www.nola.gov/nola/media/HDLC/Historic@20Districts/IrishChannel.pdf.

15 Edward Branley, "NOLA History: The Irish in New Orleans," GoNola.com, March 4, 2013: http://www.gonola.com/2013/03/04/nola-history-the-irish-in-new-orleans.html.

16 Ann Nungesser, "Irish Channel – A New Orleans Neighborhood Profile," About.Com New Orleans: http://neworleans.about.com/od/neighborhoods/a/Irish-Channel-A-New- Orleans-Neighborhood-Profile.htm.

17 www.nola.gov/nola/media/HDLC/Historic@20Districts/IrishChannel.pdf.

18 See, Friends of St. Alphonsus Church: http://www.stalphonsusneworleans.org/about.html.

19 Charles E. Nolan and Frank J. Methe, *Splendors of Faith: New Orleans Catholic Churches, 1727 – 1927*, (Baton Rouge: LSU Press, 2010), pp. 94-95. The original St. Mary's was a wooden frame chapel that in 1997 was relocated from St. Joseph Cemetary in the middle of the Garden District to Jackson Avenue.

20 Ibid., p. 95.

21 Edward Branley, "NOLA History: The Three Churches of the Irish Channel," gonola.com, October 20, 2010: http://www.gonola.com/2010/10/20/nola-history-the-three-churches- of-the-irish-channel.html.

22 Bruce Eggler, "Elderly to Start New Year in New Homes," *Times Picayune*, December 15, 1990.

23 Bruce Eggler, "Effort aims at rescue of St. Thomas Area," *Times Picayune*, May 26, 1990.

24 Bounce has been described as characterized by "call-and-response-style party" and Mardi Gras Indian chants and dance call-outs that are often hypersexual. These chants and call-outs are sung over the "Triggerman beat" that is sampled from the songs Drag Rap by the Showboys, Brown Beat by Cameron Paul, and Derek B's Rock the Beat. See, Sara Bonisteel, "Bounce 101: A Primer to the New Orleans Sound," Fox News, August 28, 2006: http://www.foxnews.com/story/2006/08/28/bounce-101-primer-to-new-orleans- sound.html.

25 Alison Fensterstock, "Cash Money 101: Lil Wayne, Birdman, and the history of Cash Money Records," Nola.com, July 17, 2015: http://www.nola.com/music/index.ssf/2015/07/lil_wayne_birdman_and_the_hist.html. The Hot Boys included Lil Wayne, Juvenile, Turk, and B.G. They released three albums, *Get It How U Live!*, *Guerilla Warfare*, and *Let 'Em Burn*. *Guerilla Warfare* achieved Platinum status within a few months of release and topped both the R&B and hip-hop charts. They also recorded a soundtrack for the film *Baller Blackin*, set in New Orleans and released in 2000. See: "Hot Boys," LilwayneHQ.com: http://www.lilwaynehq.com/hot-boys/.

26 Alison Fensterstock, "Cash Money 101."

27 See: Emily Galik and Lindsey Caruso, "Shakespeare Park," Media Nola/Tulane University: http://medianola.org/discover/place/900/Shakespeare-Park.

28 Dillard University Archives. See, "Curtailing Ailments & Conquering Adver-

NOTES (cont.)

sity: Flint-Goodridge Hospital 1896-1983," creolegen.org, August 28, 2012: http://www.creolegen.org/2012/08/28/curing-ailments-conquering-adversity-flint-goodridge-hospital-1896-1983/.

29 Ibid. The Methodist Episcopal Church founded New Orleans University in 1873 to provide African Americans–then referred to as "people of color"–an opportunity for higher education. The school charter provided for establishing a college of medicine, and in 1889 the Medical College of New Orleans University began operations.

30 Ibid.; "Flint-Goodridge Hospital of Dillard University," Waymarking.com!: http://www.waymarking.com/waymarks/WM8NJ3_Flint_Goodridge_Hospital_of_Dillard_U niversity_New_Orleans_LA.

31 Ibid.; Dillard is named after Dr. James Hardy Dillard.

32 "Curtailing Ailments & Conquering Adversity: Flint-Goodridge Hospital 1896-1983."

33 White doctors from Tulane and LSU also taught alongside them. See, "Black-owned hospital sold in New Orleans," *New York Times*, March 7, 1983: http://www.nytimes.com/1983/03/07/us/black-owned-hospital-sold-in-new- orleans.html.

34 Eric D. Griggs, M.D., "Our Story," March 5, 2014: http://ladatanews.com/news/2014/mar/05/our-story/

35 "New Orleans Hospitals: Info & Vintage Images," http://old-new-orleans.com/NO_hospitals.html.

36 Claire Perry and George Session-Perry, "Penny-A-Day Hospital," *Saturday Evening Post*, September 2, 1939, 30, 67-68.

37 "Black-owned hospital sold in New Orleans."

38 See: "The History of Flint-Goodridge Hospital of Dillard University," *Journal of the National Medical Association*, 61, no. 6 (Nov. 1969): 533-536: http://www.ncbi.nlm.nih.gov/pmc/articles/PMC2611800/.

39 "Something Spectacular," *Preservation News*, March 1, 1990: http://prn.library.cornell.edu/cgi-bin/cornell-prn?a=d&d=PRN19900301.2.2&e=-------en-20--1--txt-txIN------.

40 The quotes from individuals draw upon an interview given to Jeffrey Lee, for his commentary, "Welcome home: a renovation restores dignity and livelihood to a New Orleans community devastated by Hurricane Katrina," The Free Library: http://www.thefreelibrary.com/Welcome+home%3A+a+renovation+restores+dignity+and+livelihood+to+a+New...-a0210868069.

41 The post-Katrina renovation in 2007 required HRI to go through the same financing process and to obtain the same government approvals as the initial one.

42 Rick Jervis, "New Orleans unveils fresh model for housing the poor," *USA Today*, August 4, 2011: http://usatoday30.usatoday.com/news/nation/2011-08-03-New-Orleans-public- housing-rebuild-experiment_n.htm.

43 "Growth of the Cotton Industry," https://www.boundless.com/u-s- history/textbooks/boundless-u-s-history-textbook/the-market-revolution-1815-1840- 13/the-market-revolution-108/the-growth-of-the-cotton-industry-583-1160/. See also: Eugene R. Dattel, "Cotton and the Civil War," *Mississippi History Now*: http://mshistorynow.mdah.state.ms.us/articles/291/cotton-and-the-civil-war; and David L. Cohn, *The Life and times of King Cotton* (New York: Oxford University Press, 1956).

44 See: "1858: Cotton creates an era of economic boom for New Orleans," *Times-Picayune*, August 23, 2011: http://www.nola.com/175years/index.ssf/2011/08/1858_cotton_creates_era_of_eco.html. Today the painting hangs in the New Orleans Museum of Art.

45 "The Warehouse District Historic District Is Established," Tulane School of Architecture: New Orleans Preservation Timeline Project, March 1, 1978: http://architecture.tulane.edu/preservation-project/timeline-entry/1457.

46 Fasnacht & Brand Beerhouse Brewery (1852-1853); L. Fasnacht Beerhouse Brewery (1854-1854); L. Fasnacht Brewery (1855-1857); Fasnacht & Bros. Brewery & Beerhouse (1858-1868), Erath & Co. Brewery (1869-1871); and Fasnacht Brewery (1872-1875). See: L. Fasnacht, Beerhouse Brewery, Old Breweries: http://oldbreweries.com/breweries-by- state/louisiana/new-orleans-la-41-breweries/l-fasnacht-beerhouse-brewery-la-13-2b/. Fueled by an influx of German immigrants, New Orleans was once the brewing capital of the South. See: Dan Shea, "The Times-Picayune covers 175 years of New Orleans history," *Times Picayune*, February 2, 2012: http://www.nola.com/175years/index.ssf/2012/02/beer_the_times-picayune_covers.html. See also: Jeremy Labadie and Argyle Wolf-Knapp, *New Orleans Beer: A Hoppy History of Big Easy Brewing*, (The History Press, 2014), p. 41, and research conducted for HRI by Alain de la Villesbret.

47 Samuel Wilson and Bernard Lemann, *New Orleans Architecture: The Lower Garden District*, p. 14-15.

48 Ibid., p. 9.

49 Coleman Warner, "Layers of Time: Condo Site a History Gold Mine," *Times Picayune*, April 21, 1997.

50 Telephone interview with Shannon Dawdy, April 2014.

51 Today, all units have been converted into condos.

52 James Farwell interview with Gary Meadows by phone, October 14, 2015.

53 http://www.yelp.com/biz/cotton-mill-new-orleans.

54 http://www.yelp.com/biz/cotton-mill-apartments-new-orleans.

55 Betty Lee Nordheim, "Echoes of the Past" (Covington Independent Schools, 2002).

NOTES (cont.)

56 Peggy Scott Laborde and John Magill, *Canal Street: New Orleans Great White Way*, (New Orleans: Pelican 2006), p. 32.

57 Betty Lee Nordheim, "Echoes of the Past."

58 Joseph F. Gastright, *Gentleman Farmers to City Folks: A Study of Wallace Woods, Covington, Kentucky* (Cincinnati: Cincinnati Historical Society, 1980), accessed at: http://issuu.com/cincinnati/docs/nky-h/29. Id.

59 Peggy Scott Laborde and John Magill, *Canal Street: New Orleans Great White Way*, p. 33.

60 Nola.com collected colorful reminiscences of customers: http://www.nola.com/175years/index.ssf/2011/07/share_your_memories_dh_holmes.ht ml

61 Later, FNBC was sold. Ryan proceeded to acquire the name and started up a new one with the similar name, First NBC Bank.

62 Located at 819 Canal Street, the original building fronted on Canal Street and ran back to Iberville and Dauphine Streets.

63 "Holmes," The Department Store Museum: http://departmentstoremuseum.blogspot.com/2010/05/d-h-holmes-co-ltd.html.

64 "Government Sues American Can Company," *New York Times*, November 19, 1913: http://query.nytimes.com/mem/archive-free/pdf?res=9F0DEF-D71139E633A25753C3A9679D946296D6CF

65 Edward Branley, "NOLA History: Backatown and the Evolution of New Orleans Neighborhoods," Nola.com, November 4, 2013: http://gonola.com/2013/11/04/nola-history-backatown-and-the-evolution-of-new-orleans-neighborhoods.html. Branley has authored five books on New Orleans history, including *Legendary Locals of New Orleans* (Arcadia Publishing, 2013), available at: http://www.amazon.com/Legendary-Locals- Orleans-Edward-Branley/dp/1467100390/ref=sr_1_1?s=books&ie=UTF8&qid=1444164173&sr=1-1&keywords=Legendary+Locals+of+New+Orleans+Branley.

65 "Mid-City and Esplanade Ridge," http://www.neworleansonline.com/tools/neighborhoodguide/midcity.html.

67 "Mid-City Neighborhood Snapshot," Greater New Orleans Community Data Center: http://www.datacenterresearch.org/pre-katrina/orleans/4/45/snapshot.html.

68 Andrew Neighbours, "From Can Factory to Apartments in New Orleans," *New York Times*, March 26, 2000. The design description draws upon this story.

69 Ibid.

70 Billy Sothern, "Goodbye, St. Thomas," *The Nation*, August 27, 2007: http://www.thenation.com/article/goodbye-st-thomas#.

71 Ibid., citing *Times-Picayune*, February 23, 1941.

72 Sister Helen Prejean, *Dead Man Walking* (New York: Random House, 1993), p. 3.

73 William Julius Wilson, *The Truly Disadvantaged*, (Chicago: University of Chicago Press, 1997, 2012), p. 56.

74 Author's interview with Tony Gelderman. He is an eminent attorney in New Orleans. Kabacoff and Gelderman both wanted to achieve the same goal, although Kabacoff feels that merely selling the St. Thomas land would have generated insufficient funds. Additional funding would have been required from other sources.

75 ULI is the world's largest real estate research organization.

76 See, Michael E. Porter, *Competitive Advantage of Nations*, (New York: Free Press, 1998).

77 New Urbanism espouses a philosophy that mirrors HRI's in favoring the creation of walkable, vibrant, mixed use communities.

78 The arrangement is known as tax increment financing (TIF). The state Industrial Development Board issued an additional $20 million in tax-free bonds to cover the costs of building infrastructure—roads, sewerage and water, and utilities on the River Garden site that Morial had promised the city would pay for. Not a dollar of this benefit went to Wal-Mart or HRI. The way a TIF works is as follows: an authority issues bonds which are retired through the capture of an increment of Wal-Mart sales taxes. The bonds provide immediate cash for whatever project the city designates.

79 Author's interview with Bill Borah, October 24, 2015.

80 Ibid.

81 Constance L. Hays, "For Wal-Mart, New Orleans is Hardly the Big Easy," *New York Times*, April 27, 2003. See also, Kellie Lunney, "Dashed Hopes," *National Journal*, January 29, 2005. She talks about the desire of public housing advocates for additional subsidized units.

82 See, "GOP Square-off in South Carolina—including Ron Paul," *Huffington Post*, October 28, 2008: http://www.huffingtonpost.com/j-neffinger-g-macnicol-d-shea-and-r- sklar/liveblog-gop-squareoff-in_b_81003.html.

83 This was stated in a letter to Pres Kabacoff.

84 Dr. Silas Lee, survey of public opinions and attitudes as to St. Thomas & Wal-Mart, September 10, 2001. And 90% of respondents said they or a family member shop at a local Wal-Mart.

85 Andras Duany, *Suburban Nation*, (New York: North Point Press, 2010).

86 Greg Thomas, "Home Grown," *Times Picayune*, July 25, 2004.

87 Initial planning contemplated allocating 50 percent of subsidized affordable housing. Economically the final allocation was essential to make the project feasible.

NOTES (cont.)

88 Holly Miller, "Magazine rents skyrockets after River Garden becomes reality," *City Business*, August 30, 2004.

89 Christopher Tidmore, "St. Thomas Reborn . . .", *Louisiana Weekly*, November 29, 2004: http://www.freedomworks.org/content/louisiana-weeklys-inside-political-track.

90 Molly Reid, "St. Thomas reborn in River Garden," *Times-Picayune*, November 1, 2007: http://blog.nola.com/times-picayune/2007/11/st_thomas_reborn_in_river_gard.html.

91 Doug McCash, "Gentrification of Bywater and St. Claude Avenue was sped up by flood and 2008 economic slump," NOLA.com, January 25, 2013: http://www.nola.com/arts/index.ssf/2013/01/the_long_term_gentrification_o.htm.

92 Ibid.

93 Ibid.

94 Doug MacCash, "Bywater Art Lofts 2, an $11.3 million investment, holding grand opening tonight," NOLA.com, October 12, 2012: http://www.nola.com/arts/index.ssf/2012/10/bywater_art_lofts_2_an_113_mil.html.

95 See, Ron Nyren, *Urban Land*, "Preserving the Past," Nov-Dec 2011.

96 Ibid.

97 See, "Standard Life Building," Mississippi Historic Preservation Curriculum: http://www.mississippiheritage.com/curriculum/MHT%20Curriculum%20_%2015%20E xercise%208.pdf

98 Cheryl Lassweter, "Standard Life Building opens for apartment tenants," msnewsnow, February 18, 2013: http://www.msnewsnow.com/story/13083728/standard-life- building-opens-for-apartment-tenants.

99 Jennifer Dockery, "Multimillion Dollar Renovation Revives State Capitol," *Journal of Tax Credits*, August 2010.

100 Carol Pulitzer, "Blue Plate lofts get artistic touch," *Times Picayune*, June 13, 2012: http://www.nola.com/nolavie/index.ssf/2012/06/blue_plate_lofts_get_artistic.html. Hernandez is a remarkable woman. She was chosen as one of only thirty-three participants from applicants around the world to learn how to collaborate on projects like Blue Plate. Ibid.

101 See, Carol Pulitzer, "When the stars align," Nolavie, June 13, 2012: http://nolavie.com/when-the-stars-align-64399/

102 See, Roger Hahn, "Blue Plate Artist Lofts," *Country Roads*, July (2013): http://www.countryroadsmagazine.com/culture/profiles-people-places/blue-plate-artist-lofts.

103 Elizabeth Rush, "As the seas rise, managing retreat along New York City's Coast," *New Republic*, October 25, 2015.

104 Carol Pulitzer, "When the stars align."

105 A Section 3 employee is an occupant or prior occupant of public housing.

106 PILOT: Payment in Lieu of Taxes. The program allows a below-market tax bill and spurs development.

107 "Developers see apartment potential in CBD office space:" http://www.larryschedler.com/developers-see-apartment-potential-in-cbd-office-space/.

108 Interview with Kurt Weigle, October 20, 2015.

109 Sarah Chase, "Former Texaco Building Set To Open As Senior Housing," NOLA.com, March 5, 2014: http://nola.curbed.com/archives/2014/03/05/former-texaco-building-set-to- open-as-senior-housing.php.

110 Interview with Mike Valentino, October 13, 2015.

111 Interview with Kurt Weigle, October 20, 2015.

112 Katy Reckdahl, "Iberville demolition marks end of an era," *Advocate*, July 30, 2013.

113 "Culture & Change: Black History in America," http://teacher.scholastic.com/activities/bhistory/history_of_jazz.htm

114 Katy Reckdahl, "Iberville demolition marks end of an era."

115 Cain Burdeau, "New Orleans' Post-Katrina Gentrification is Touchy," Associated Press, August 28, 2012: http://bigstory.ap.org/article/new-orleans-post-katrina-gentrification- touchy.

116 Nora Goddard, "The Destruction of Public Housing in New Orleans," nolatourguy.com, November 27, 2012: http://www.nolatourguy.com/public-housing/.

117 Ibid.; Katy Reckdahl, "Iberville demolition marks end of an era."

118 Wade Rathke, "The Real Danger in Treme is HUD's Choice Neigbhorhoods and Heritage Tourism," July 25, 2012: http://chieforganizer.org/2012/07/25/the-real-danger-in-treme-is-hud%E2%80%99s-choice-neighborhoods-and-heritage-tourism/.

119 "New Orleans receives money to redevelop Iberville housing complex," CityBusiness/Associated Press, September 1, 2011. The Mayor reiterated the point on August 19, 2015 in a speech to the National Press Club in Washington. See: https://www.youtube.com/watch?v=vIzgbGFtp_8.

120 Cain Burdeau, "New Orleans' Post-Katrina Gentrification is Touchy."

121 The HUD Choice Neighborhoods Implementation Grant.

122 Pres Kabacoff observes that New Orleans has far too few affordable housing units. "There's a waiting list of 17,000 now, and we're advised that if you re-opened that list, another 50,000 would be added."

123 See: Raj Chetty and Nathaniel Hendren, "The Impacts of Neighborhoods on

NOTES (cont.)

Intergenerational Mobility," April 2015: http://www.equality-of-opportunity.org/images/nbhds_exec_summary.pdf; David Leonhardt, Amanda Cox and Claire Miller, "An Atlas of Upward Mobility Shows Paths Out of Poverty," *New York Times*, May 4, 2015: http://www.nytimes.com/2015/05/04/upshot/an-atlas-of-upward-mobility-shows-paths-out-of-poverty.html?abt=0002&abg=0&_r=1. For a contra view: Sarah Sloat, "For Boys, Moving to a Wealthier Neighborhood Is as Traumatic as Going to War," *New Republic*, March 5, 2014: http://www.newrepublic.com/article/116886/boys-report-ptsd-when-they-move-richer-neighborhoods. The story observes that boys who move into more affluent neighborhoods report higher rates of depression and conduct disorder than their female peers. See also: "Moving to Opportunity (MTO) for Fair Housing Demonstration Program," U.S. Dept. of Housing and Urban Development: http://www.nber.org/mtopublic/.

124 David Leonhardt, Amanda Cox and Claire Miller, "An Atlas of Upward Mobility Shows Paths Out of Poverty." At this writing, both Democrat Hillary Clinton and Republican Jeb Bush have signaled that mobility will be a central theme of their 2016 Presidential campaigns. Ibid. President Barack Obama's Secretary of Housing and Urban Development has indicated that funding will be reallocated so that some people moving to more expensive neighborhoods would receive larger vouchers for subsidized housing so that they can afford to live in such neighborhoods. Ibid. See also, Robert Steutville, "Numbers don't lie: HOPE VI has worked wonders," Better Cities & Towns, June 1, 2004: http://bettercities.net/article/numbers- don%E2%80%99t-lie-hope-vi-has-worked-wonders. Steutville argues that the HOPE VI program is a "great achievement" and that "census tracts with HOPE VI projects perform better in every category than all poverty-stricken neighborhoods." See also, Robert Steuteville, "Who Wants the Towers Back?" *Better Cities & Towns*, Sept-Oct (2013): http://bettercities.net/article/who-wants-towers-back-20691. Here Steutville observes that thanks to HOPE VI, and quoting architect Dan Solomon, "with help from new urbanist designers, the projects were replaced with 'sensible, straightforward, sometimes even beautiful neighborhoods,' the kind that used to be the basic fabric of American cites." See, Dan Solomon, *Global City Blues*, (Washington: Island Press, 3rd. ed., 2003). These studies show that HRI's operations reflect best practices in conception and management of former public housing developments.

125 Author interview with Kurt Weigle, October 20, 2015.

126 "Bank to Open New Building," *Dallas Morning News*, May 31, 1964.

127 Jack Fink, "New Project Lends to Downtown Dallas Living," CBSDFW.Com, May 29, 2014: http://dfw.cbslocal.com/2014/05/29/new-project-lends-to-downtown-dallas-living/.

128 "New Orleans-based HRI Properties Launches Reconstruction of Historic LTV Building in Downtown Dallas," Yahoo, May 29, 2014: http://finance.yahoo.com/news/orleans- based-hri-properties-launches-204300126.html.

IMAGE CREDITS

HRi Properties: 8, right; 19; 28; 32; 37; 38, both; 39; 40; 45; 46, all; 47, all; 48; 56; 61; 62, all; 63, all; 64, both; 65, both; 72, all; 73, all; 80, all; 82, both; 83; 84; 86; 87; 89; 90, right; 91, all; 92; 93, bottom right; 96; 97; 100, both; 104; 105, both; 106; 107, all; 108; 110, all; 112; 115; 117; 118, all except lower right; 119, all; 120; 121, all; 123; 124, both; 125; 126; 127, all; 128; 130; 132; 134; 135; 136, all; 137, all; 143; 146; 148; 151, all; 154, top; 155, all; 161, all except top left; 163; 168; 177, all; 179, all; 180; 182, both; 183, all; 187; 188; 194; 200.

John Slaughter: front cover; title page; copyright page; 8, left; 15; 18; 21; 22; 26; 27 35, inset; 36; 42; 44, both; 49; 50; 54; 55; 60; 74; 75; 76; 78; 79; 81; 88; 102; 103; 109; 111; 113; 114; 118, lower right; 139; 140; 142, both; 150; 152; 153; 154, bottom; 156; 160; 161, top left; 162; 164; 172; 173; 174; 175; 176; 178; 186, both; 191, both; 193; 195; 196; 197; 198; 199, 201.

The Historic New Orleans Collection, Charles L. Franck Studio Collection: 24, acc. no. 1979.325.3015; 35, acc. no. 1979.89.7237; 41, acc. no. 1979.325.1030; 43, acc. no. 1979.325.1024; 53, acc. no. 1979.325.803; 59, acc. no. 1979.325.2892; 71, acc. no. 1979.325.1658; 131, acc. no. 1979.325.2898; 141, acc. no. 1979.325.2898; 149, acc. no. 1994.94.2.2057; 157, acc. no. 1979.325.584; 159, acc. no. 1979.325.5057; 166-167, acc. no. 1979.89.7578.

James D. Wilson, Jr.: 20; 23; 33; 34; 51; 52; 66; 68; 69; 70; 90, left; 98, top left; 98, bottom right; 133.

Cheryl Gerber: 14, 138; 144, all; 145; 192.

New Orleans Public Library, Louisiana Division: 95; 165.

Brenda Boettner: 189.

Tate Nations: 122.

Library of Congress: 6.

Franklin D. Roosevelt Library and Museum: 94.

National Archives and Records Administration: 93, top left.

Praise for *Revitalizing Cities: The HRI Vision*

"One would be hard-pressed to identify a firm that has had a more profound influence on the built environment of modern New Orleans than HRI, be it through the adaptive reuse of landmark historical structures or the New Urbanist redevelopment of public housing. Revitalizing Cities *tells that story from the inside—the history, the philosophies, the people behind them, and most of all the architecture and cityscapes that resulted. It's an important read for anyone interested in urbanism, in New Orleans and beyond, and I highly recommend it."*

- Richard Campanella,
Urban Geographer and Author,
Tulane University

"A fascinating book about one of this nation's most imaginative, cutting edge companies in revitalizing cities. HRI is a leader in creating mixed used, mixed income housing in a city that is rooted in cultural, ethnic, and racial diversity. Its achievements in historic renovation rank in the top-tier in the nation."

- Moon Landrieu,
former Mayor of New Orleans and
former Secretary of Housing & Urban Development

"I first met Pres and HRI in 1991, as they sought financing for the conversion of the empty former site of New Orleans's largest department store. A lovely, historic building on the outside, a disaster on the inside. HRI's creativity, vision, and economic savvy turned that distressed property on world famous Canal Street into a beautiful, historic, economically viable hotel; in so doing began the revitalization of the New Orleans core. Pres and HRI are a team that produces magic."

- Ashton J. Ryan Jr.,
President, First NBC Bank

"HRI's work has led to a renaissance in downtown New Orleans. Its work is truly outstanding. Their work, which this informative and highly readable book describes, is an important contribution to the vibrancy of downtown New Orleans and other cities."

- Joseph C. Canizaro,
Owner, Columbus Properties and
former President, Urban Land Institute

"An important, engaging book. HRI's renovations of the King Edward hotel and the Standard Life building in downtown Jackson were stunning. HRI is a unique company and what it does and how it does it is a must read for anyone interested in bringing historic cities alive again."

- Haley Barbour,
former Governor of Mississippi

"HRI builds difficult projects the hard way—by caring for the city and its people while still keeping an eye firmly on the profit line. This alchemy was responsible for most of the places we now love. This book is evidence that one outfit at least still knows how to do it."

- Andrés Duany, FAIA, CNU
Founding Partner, DPZ LLC and
founder of the Congress for the New Urbanism

"Pres Kabacoff and Edward Boettner were among the earliest visionaries, and their company, HRI, has led the revitalization movement in New Orleans and many other cities across the country. This book is both a great read and offers terrific insights into how a great company can make a difference in restoring and adapting historic properties to give new vitality to neighborhoods and communities."

- Ron Filson,
Dean and Professor Emeritus,
Tulane University School of Architecture

"A well-told book and great read that tells the story of an innovative, fascinating, company whose exceptional work brings new life to historic neighborhoods and cities."

- Charles C. Teamer Sr.,
Vice Chairman of the Board, First NBC Bank

"HRI should be considered one of the top corporate citizens in America with its mission and proven success in revitalizing cities. HRI has repeatedly demonstrated that preservation and adaptive reuse in our forgotten downtowns can be profitable endeavors. . . . Pres Kabacoff's driving force for excellence in design and redesign have regenerated economies in St. Louis, Dallas, Jackson, as well as homebased New Orleans, where his footprint is larger than any other in multiple historic places. The domino impact of HRI's transformative work has brought dazzling change in many dark corners of our nation."

- Dana Crawford,
Urban Neighborhoods, Inc.,

"A thought-provoking book, and a must read for anyone who recognizes that historic cities thrive when they are revitalized and re-energized. HRI is a national leader in historic revitalization. The book also tells the vital story of how it worked in public/private partnerships to create real opportunities for a diverse population through mixed used, mixed income housing."

- Marc H. Morial,
CEO, National Urban League and
former Mayor of New Orleans